Life Untwisted

Targeting Your Potential With A Fearless Attitude

Dannye and John Dean Williamsen

Published by:
Williamsen Publications
Cordova, TN 38018

http://www.WilliamsenPublications.com

All rights reserved. No part of this book may be reproduced or transmitted in any form or by any means, electronic or mechanical, including photocopying, recording, or by any other information storage and retrieval system, without written permission from the authors.

©2014 Dannye Williamsen and John Dean Williamsen

The individual chapters in this book were originally written between the years of 1998 and 2014 by the authors of this book.

DEDICATION

Life Untwisted is dedicated
to all the joys and heartaches
that have accompanied our journeys so far.

Table of Contents

Dedication 3
Introduction 11
PART ONE 13
Developing A Fearless attitude 13
   BUILDING A FOUNDATION 15
      ▶ Be Receptive To New Ideas 17
         Being Teachable Opens Doors 17
      ▶ Determine Your Perspective 21
         Become A Driver, Not A Passenger 21
         Choose Your Own Reality 25
         How Do You See Yourself? 27
      ▶ Understand The Workings Of Your Inner World 29
         What Determines The Life You Are Living? 29
         The Discipline of Choices 31
         Blind Vs. Understanding Faith 33
         Magnetic Center: The Spiritual Perspective 37
         Personality: Your Medium Of Exchange 43
         The Impact of Personality On Your Essence 45
      ▶ Utilize Spiritual Tools 49
         Three Tools For A Better Life 49
         Self-Observation: A Spiritual Discipline 53
         Self-Remembering: Disengaging From Your Roles 57

The Nine Basic Steps of Meditation 61
Avoid Mind Candy 65
HEALING 67
▶ Break Old Patterns..69
Does It Feel Like You're In A Rut? 69
Is Procrastination Your Bedfellow? 75
Do You Detour Rather Than Change?..............................77
Perfectionism Is Highly Over-Rated!................................79
You Are Absolutely Good Enough 81
Denial and the Dance Of Chaos 83
Boomerang Effect Keeps You Running In Place 91
Break Out Of Your Shell 95
Take A Chance On Off-Road Exploring............................99
Overcome The Conditioning In Your Life 103
▶ Let's Talk About Subpersonalities...105
Is There A War Going On Inside You?.............................105
Recognizing Your Uniqueness Is The Key......................109
▶ Express Yourself 115
Jumpstart Your Self-Esteem 115
7 Ways To Fire Up Your Life 117
The Power Of Purpose 119
▶ Pay Attention To Your Feelings 123
Accessing The Magic Energy 123
Useless, Unnecessary Suffering..125
7 Sure-Fire Ways To Lose Everything 129

Tips For Handling Stress Or Burnout 131
The Real Power Behind Your Thoughts 135
Your Feelings Will Beat You To The Punch Every Time 137
Put Your Energy Where It Counts! 139

STRATEGIES 143

◉ Exploit Your Weaknesses 145
If It Doesn't Destroy You, It Will Make You Stronger ... 145
Ready-Aim-Fire 149
Believe In Your Good 151

◉ Set Goals And Give Intention 153
Getting Off On The Right Foot With Your Goals 153
Why Motivates Better Than *How-To* 157
How An Idea Can Change Your Life 159
Attracting And Harmonizing With Your Desires 161
Stop Groaning! It's Good For You! 163
Use Wisdom To Achieve Balance 167

◉ Step Out Into The Unknown 171
Looking Over Your Shoulder 171
What Is The Color Of Your Universe? 173
Risking: Living Without A Net 177

◉ Redefine Your Life 181
Even Baby-Boomers Can Redefine Their Lives 181
Can De-cluttering Redefine You? 185

REVIEW QUESTIONS: Developing A Fearless Attitude 189

PART TWO	195
TARGETING YOUR POTENTIAL	195
CREATIVE PROCESS	197
Yes, Virginia, There Is A System In Place	199
Quit Thinking About It … Do Something!	201
Where's Your Passion?	203
Self-help Programs Vs. The Creative Process	205
7 Tips For Finding A Quality Self-help Program	209
VISIONS FOR LIFE AND BUSINESS	213
▶ Setting The Stage	213
Hump? What Hump?	213
Make Sure Your Dream Doesn't Become A Nightmare	217
Develop The State Of Mind For Prosperity	221
Skyrocket The Impact Of Your Talent	225
Rekindle Your Passion	227
▶ Leadership	229
Dealing With Crises	229
Is Your Business Partnership Working?	235
Ethics: Do They Matter?	239
Your View Of Your Business Sets Its Tone	249
Create Goals That Lead To Success	251
Evaluate Your Business For Success	253
The Success Spiral	259
RELATIONSHIPS IN LIFE AND BUSINESS	263
▶ Friends, Family, and Significant Others	263

Fear: A Milestone 263
Who Is The Real Problem In Your Relationships? 265
You Know How You Are… 271
3 Ways To Survive Going Home For The Holidays 273
Building Strong Relationships 277
What Happens When You Mourn? 287
◉ Co-workers/Associates 289
Creating A Sense Of Family In The Workplace 289
◉ Networking...295
Are You A Networker, A Gatherer, Or A Collector? 295
A Higher View Of Networking 299
Set Priorities To Network Effectively 301
Fitting In: Small Group Dynamics 305
REVIEW QUESTIONS: Targeting Your Potential 311
Conclusion...315
About The Authors 317

INTRODUCTION

> *"Life can become so twisted
> at times that we lose the balance
> in our lives and don't even know it
> until we land face down
> in the garbage we've accumulated.
> When we untwist our lives,
> the walls become halls."*
> - Life Untwisted

In trying to live our lives, we inadvertently get things twisted around. We lose sight of what's important for our spiritual growth and what's inconsequential. Of course, nothing is really inconsequential because lessons are there to be learned regardless. However, it is still important for us to prioritize the people, the actions, the feelings, the thoughts in our lives because most of us tend to turn our worlds upside down. We make the least important the most important and vice versa. We carry the residue of experiences around with us that we should have released long ago and let them rule our lives.

In order to live a happier life, we must learn how to develop a fearless attitude and how to target our potential. Each of these undertakings involves certain areas of work. To develop a fearless attitude, we must work on building a foundation, healing, and strategies, each of which also include many areas of focus. To target our potential, we must understand the creative process, develop visions for our life and business as well as learn how to create better relationships.

Each of these chapters were written at different times before finding a home within the pages of this book – all for the purpose of untwisting our lives.

PART ONE

DEVELOPING A FEARLESS ATTITUDE

BUILDING A FOUNDATION

"Most people are about as happy as they make up their minds to be."
– Abraham Lincoln

You are the architect of your life, and because you are, it is up to you the colors you choose for painting your experiences, and it is up to you how you design the rooms in the house that is your life – whether you choose an open plan, a free-flowing plan, or one that chops your life up into discrete pieces.

Because you are the architect of your life, you determine just how happy you will be with the house you're building that is your life experience.

Building a strong foundation for this house by tending your spiritual growth is as important as it is when building a house. Unfortunately, we often skip the preparatory steps when we move toward a goal of any kind because they often seem boring or too laborious. If, however, you are sincere about wanting to straighten out your life, you must be willing to invest energy in every step of the process.

Quite often in these chapters, you will find us viewing life from the perspective of an entrepreneur. The information is just as applicable to you whether you work for someone else or don't work at all. You still have goals, just like an entrepreneur does. The principles apply even if your goal involves organizing events for a volunteer organization or organizing your home. So don't shut down just because some of the examples don't fit your life exactly.

◐ Be Receptive To New Ideas

BEING TEACHABLE OPENS DOORS

Everyone has been told at one time or another that you should "act as if," that you should always appear confident because no one will believe in you if you don't. All of this is true. However, sometimes you can take it too far. You try so hard to appear that you know what you're doing that you are no longer teachable. When this happens, you are in deep trouble.

At one time or the other, everyone is selling either an idea, a product, or a service. Usually, their knowledge is skewed in the direction of that one thing. Even when you are dealing with family or friends, you will often find yourself selling an idea about how something should be accomplished. You have probably thought a great deal about this idea and developed a lot of passion about its worthiness. Are you open to suggestions or other ideas?

Let's consider someone in business. If you have a carpet cleaning business, you probably know more about carpets and cleaning fluids than I would ever want to know! But, what do you know about marketing? What do you know about accounting? What do you know about managing employees? The chances are that your knowledge base is considerably less in every area but the one for which you have a passion. This is not unusual. As a matter of fact, most people's knowledge is domain-specific. It is expected.

So what's the problem? To help you understand, let me share a definition of an entrepreneur straight out of Wall Street with you. David L. Scott in "Wall Street Words," defined entrepreneur as *"a risk-taker who has the skills and initiative to establish a business."* This seems to be the definition so many people try to emulate.

The problem with this is that it implies we already have *all* the necessary skills. Consequently, how can we possibly be considered an entrepreneur if we have to ask for help? How can we possibly admit to a shortcoming in any area of expertise? As a result, we try harder to portray ourselves as an entrepreneur than we do as a carpet cleaner or a maker of jewelry or whatever.

Even when we're talking about interacting with family or friends regarding a project or an idea, we often push to prove ourselves capable and intelligent and lose sight of the reason for the idea in the first place.

We Can Never Be Happy And Successful Unless We Remain Teachable

Even if you have passable knowledge in all the operational areas we mentioned earlier, there is always someone who has valuable knowledge you could use to improve your business or your idea. No one can keep up with the rapid expanse of information and/or technology today unless these are your passion *AND* your focus.

Why is it important for you to remain teachable?

- Trying to do everything yourself when you are constantly having to educate yourself in new areas is a sure-fire road to burnout.

- Refusing to open yourself up to others' ideas or experiences means that you have to do most things the hard way.

- If you're not teachable, you won't learn from the experiences you have in life, which makes your life a merry-go-round of reruns.

- One more thing: Being afraid to allow others to take the reins in certain areas of your business or your life indicates a lack of trust on your part.

But, what does this have to do with being teachable? It is an opportunity for you to learn to trust. Nothing teaches trust more quickly than the experience of delegating, and the rewards can be immense!

So, it doesn't really matter if you're a business owner or not, in trying to be successful in your life, allow yourself the privilege of being *a person who organizes and manages any enterprise, whether in life or business, with considerable initiative and willingness to risk.* Notice that it doesn't say anything about doing it all or knowing it all!

So enjoy the process of learning, delegating, teaching, and succeeding!

⏵ Determine Your Perspective

BECOME A DRIVER, NOT A PASSENGER

What is the primary difference between a driver and a passenger? The driver has control. He can choose where to go and how to get there. The passenger goes along for the ride, but the thrill and the satisfaction of navigating the course and determining the destination is not part of his experience except vicariously.

Do you take charge of your experiences or do you let others call the shots? Do you sit quietly on the side, perhaps even offer advice, but never take the wheel? If you answered "yes," I'll also bet that you have a lot of dreams you never expect to be more than just dreams.

If you do want to make your dreams come true, you have to sit behind the wheel and navigate your own course. It's not easy. There will be moments when you feel like a failure. You will make turns that cause you to detour from your planned path, but it's the only chance you have of reaching your goals. No one is going to bring them to you. You have to make the journey yourself.

When you set a goal, it's imperative to understand there will be resistance. For every action, there is an equal and opposite reaction. The resistance could be an "in your face" event, or it may be more subtle. It may just be those voices in your head that tell you all the reasons you can't do this. Setbacks are not negative events, however, and neither are the voices. The *setbacks* are reflections of attitudes that are within you—attitudes that drew those kinds of experiences to you. The *voices* are those attitudes inside you stepping up to the microphone in an effort to maintain the status quo. How you deal with resistance is an important part of your journey. If you fall victim to the setbacks or the voices, you will start making excuses about why your goal is out of your reach or why you're not meant to have it.

When dealing with resistance, remember to keep your eye on your goal so that you don't get too far off course. Setbacks are your opportunity to change your life—to meet those old ideas you have about yourself and move past them without letting them slow you down too much. Don't think it will necessarily be easy though. Confronting these attitudes means tearing down parts of your belief system. This can be scary. After all, you've spent your whole life creating and embracing these beliefs. Everything you've done has been supported by them. You may even feel a sense of loyalty to them. If they say you don't have the talent to accomplish your new goal, going ahead with it could feel like a betrayal or just a silly escapade that will eventually embarrass you and prove that your old beliefs are right.

It takes courage and persistence to confront the resistance you meet when you set a goal. It also requires directed movement. Do you have a map in your mind showing various ways to get from where you are now to where you want to be? If you've never been somewhere before, a map is advantageous. It's just as true when you set out to reach a goal. Unfortunately, people who speak about goal-setting often gloss over this part as if beginning the journey is the easiest aspect of reaching one's goal. Actually, it isn't. I put it right up there with the first time you get behind the wheel of a car and have to turn left onto a busy highway from a parking lot. It seems impossible, and you put the car in reverse several times to back up and look for a better way out. Don't be discouraged if it feels like you don't have a clue in the beginning. Most people don't. It's only afterward when they've figured it out that clarity arrives, and they no longer remember being unsure of the steps along the way.

Be sure to *stretch yourself*! If you don't, you will choose goals consistent with your beliefs about yourself. Such goals encounter little resistance and are easy to achieve. Stretching yourself increases your confidence as you meet setbacks so that you can continue on. Even the nature of your goals may change. You may choose the scenic route rather than the freeway because you understand that the journey is more important than the destination. When you finally do reach your goal, you will already be making plans for the next journey. You will never be a passenger again!

CHOOSE YOUR OWN REALITY

Giving in to "reality" is so easy. The authorities assure us that they are the experts. These authorities can be doctors, teachers, parents, employers. No matter who they are, their beliefs are based on bodies of knowledge that do not take into account your personal resolve—your personal creative power.

Giving in to their proclamations about your capabilities, your future, only affirms their version of your reality. For those familiar with spiritual psychology, this is an accepted statement. It seems reasonable. It *is* reasonable. It is true. Unfortunately for most people, however, it is extremely difficult to overcome the pressures of these authority figures in your lives. If a doctor tells you something, it is a little scary to choose a different path. If a teacher or a parent says you don't have the intelligence to be what you desire, it can make you hesitant to keep pursuing your dream.

Always *consider* the information others give you, but never let them be your only source of information. This is always true, no matter what the circumstances. Even if you decide to follow an "expert's" advice, *let the decision be yours, not theirs.* You know yourself better than they do. Weigh their advice against your own research, your own knowledge of your strengths and weaknesses. Then make the decision about what is best for you.

There are some situations in life where we have pre-existing ideas about what it will be like, and we are disappointed or discouraged by the actual reality and end up allowing the authorities and the situations to color our futures.

One example: Many think that college is a place where the professors and students are genuinely interested in exploring knowledge together, and the professors will be intimately interested in your goals. This is rarely true and has been disappointing for many students. Professors are people who have a job. Rarely do they attempt to engage their students in intellectual pursuits beyond the class lectures and project assignments. If students want to succeed, they must drive themselves. It won't be a group effort. You must not allow the indifferent atmosphere to determine your choices about your future.

Another example: When you are stricken with an illness of some kind, you may think that the doctors are really interested in your getting well. You think they will take everything about you into account. I see this often on TV, but it is not reality. The truth is that doctors generally follow prescribed protocols, schedule the tests, and make judgments. Trying to give them information or get information is difficult at best.

So, if you want to take charge of your recovery, you have to demand the facts and do your own research to see if there are confounding variables they're ignoring. Then discuss the situation with your doctor. You may have to force the issues because often they don't like to be questioned, but it is your responsibility to find out. Then you have to make the decision whether the benefits of the medications you're taking are worth the risk of the side effects. No one should make that choice but you.

The important point of these examples is that whatever the situation, the final decision should be YOUR decision, not the expert's. You may choose to follow their advice. That's fine. Just make sure that you get all the facts and inform yourself about the positive and negative effects of your decision. Then it is YOU determining your future, not someone else.

Developing A Fearless Attitude

How Do You See Yourself?

Have you ever heard the expression that *God expresses through me as me*? I believe this to be a very important statement. However, its value to us in our spiritual journeys is like everything else we encounter: what we receive from the information depends on our vantage point or our awareness at that moment.

At this point in my life, I have been intently examining my place in this expression of God that we know as the Universe and the expression that I experience as me. I believe that, like Pierre Teilhard said, we are spiritual beings having a human experience, not humans having a spiritual experience. Having accepted this truth, I am asking myself how I fit into this idea. How can my personality, my humanness, as it interacts with the world around me express this truth?

If I am indeed God in expression, what is my role in this process? How do I experience the reality of the oneness that is God, the oneness of all things? This thought process requires that I examine and harmonize many concepts, such as free will, humility, desire, being created in the image and likeness, co-creation, and many more.

Recently I heard someone say that the difference between a spiritual person (regardless of their religion) and a carnal person (also regardless of their religion) is that a spiritual person does what they do for God, and a carnal person does what they do for themselves. Each has a different vantage point for their lives.

A carnal person may do all the "right things" demanded by their religion or society to qualify as a "good" person, but it does not accomplish what they think it will. It is not about WHAT you do; it is about WHY you do it. You may do what you do out of fear that hell will be waiting for you if you don't. You may do what you do because you want to look good while you're on this earth. Either way, it is the WHY that is impacting your consciousness in a less than desirable way.

So, if the carnal approach is not ideal, what does it mean to be a spiritual person? It doesn't mean that you don't adhere to any particular religious tenets. It means that you recognize your role in the creative expressions of God. I believe that we were each endowed with certain attributes and talents from God when we were born into this world (*made in the image and likeness*). As a result, God has the opportunity to express through these unique combinations, which we call human beings. This is the main reason for the life each of us experiences here.

Free will, however, gives us the opportunity to make choices which impact the clear expression of God flowing through us. This free will combines with our lack of humility and our fears to build up filters or obstacles to this flow so that we are no longer expressing the clarity that is trying to flow through us.

We lose touch with the inherent knowledge that **our role is to be a channel for God's expression** by using our unique combination of attributes and talents. This is difficult to swallow for most of us because our vantage point is *of the world*. In other words, we believe that our good comes from the world, and it is the things of the world that determine our value. In truth, our value is not in question. What really matters is our consciousness, our understanding of our co-creative role with God in this wonderful experience we call life.

If I see myself as a channel through which God expresses, using my unique combination of attributes and talents, then the energy I have been investing in building up my ego and in following the expectations of the world will no longer be available to support those false ideas. My energy will be properly invested, and I will experience the joy and prosperity that has been patiently waiting for me to look at myself with a clearer understanding of my role as a co-creator with God.

◐ Understand The Workings Of Your Inner World

WHAT DETERMINES THE LIFE YOU ARE LIVING?

You came to this planet to do one thing ... **increase your consciousness!** At the end of your time on this earth, the level of your success in life is not evaluated by the worldly things you have acquired, but rather on how much you have grown in consciousness.

What is consciousness? Consciousness is the sum total of your thoughts, feelings, and impressions. It is these thoughts, feelings, and impressions within your mind that produce the quality of life you're living. Your consciousness is who you are at the moment.

How much do you actually know about yourself? Are you really aware of why you do certain things and react in certain ways? Do you know why you find yourself connected to certain jobs, people or experiences?

The truth is, you would be the exception rather than the rule if you possessed this depth of awareness. Very few have even the slightest knowledge about the internal forces that motivate them. Don't bother asking what the level of your consciousness is. Look around you! You are living it! Your health, your degree of wealth, and your social world are all expressing your consciousness at this moment.

How do you change your consciousness if you don't like what's going on in your life? Well, first, you have to recognize that that there is a creative power which connects your thoughts, feelings, and impressions to the experiences you are having in the world. This creative power is the mechanism through which you are able to effect change in your world.

However, the first step that's required is changing the sum total of those thoughts, feelings, and impressions in your mind, in other words, your consciousness. You have to shift your perspective if you want to create different experiences in your life. The difficult part of changing your consciousness is that it is not just the obvious attitudes that impact the mechanism. The subtleties in your subconscious mind have just as much power to create your life.

Most of your problems come from what lurks in the dark, unnoticed areas of your mind. It is the unknown elements within you that can, and often do, sabotage your good intentions, and destroy your dreams. Unless you bring them out and expose them to the light of this higher understanding, you will never see how they are connected with the difficulties you are having. Growth in consciousness is achieved through the process of becoming aware of *all* the thoughts, feelings, and impressions you hold in your mental world and then dealing with them.

THE DISCIPLINE OF CHOICES

Your life is one set of choices after another. To experience the life you say you want, however, is not such a simple process as saying, "I'll take that!" Choosing requires discipline, and discipline involves knowing what you really desire, using discernment in making your choice, and being aware of what's necessary to achieve permanent prosperity.

One issue that often derails the manifestation of one's desire is pushing to manifest your desire before you have the consciousness for it. This leads to problems at worst or temporary prosperity at best. You'll give meaning to the expression that "anything you have to fight to get, you'll have to fight to keep."

There are a lot of programs and approaches out there that promise instant results. This is all well and good if you already have the consciousness for prosperity. However, if you suffer from self-doubt [which is likely or you wouldn't be searching for a way to access your prosperity], failing to build the proper mental and spiritual foundation to support these new ideas will eat away at your prosperity, and you will find yourself right back where you started or constantly fighting to maintain. No program that avoids the discipline of metanoia can promise you permanent prosperity. Most quick fix programs depend on animating your Id, your desire for immediate gratification, which effectively walks around your need to build a proper foundation to support your desire.

We're told that when seeking to manifest a desire, most of the work must be done within first. This disturbs a lot of people because they feel this means they should sit back and wait. Actually, it simply means that you must establish the right perspective—view your world from the proper vantage point—before making choices and acting on them. If you see the world as the source of your supply for this desire, if that is your vantage point, your ability to manifest and maintain your desire is compromised. If you see God as the source of your supply, you are in vibrational harmony with permanent prosperity and the unfolding of your desire.

The bottom line is that once you have made a choice about what you desire, the most important choice you have left is whether to look inward or outward for the source of your supply. This is the choice that determines the permanence of your prosperity and, ultimately, the quality of your life.

BLIND VS. UNDERSTANDING FAITH

In the audio book *It's Your Move!* we spoke about the Creative Process and the work required for change. We were primarily addressing a Change in your Being. The Creative Process, however, does not apply only to **changes in being**. It also applies to what you do and have. Is there a difference between *doing and having* and the act of *changing your being*? Yes. With doing and having, it is possible to use blind faith to manifest what you desire. For changes in being, you must have understanding faith. To explain the difference between blind and understanding faith, I first need to describe how they fit into your experiences.

Worldly Level of Your Life

Your individual life is a hierarchy of simultaneous experiences. There is a **worldly** level of experiences and a **spiritual** level. On the worldly level, your desires are directed primarily toward *doing* something or *having* something. Conscious direction of the Creative Process works quite well at this level because focus and action are the primary components of success.

Spiritual Level of Your Life

The worldly experiences are designed to turn you inward. So, when you reach a point where all the *doing and having* isn't enough, you turn inward toward your spirituality. Your attention is now focused on *changing your being*. The effort to change your being, unlike your efforts to do and have, is a life-long endeavor, requiring conscious attention and hard, often painful, internal work.

Blind faith is all that's really necessary at the *doing and having* level of life. You are only focused on what you want. You use the Creative Process to zoom in and clarify your desire. Then you move your feet.

To change your being, you must be working at the spiritual level. It is at this level that **understanding faith** comes into play. Through your experiences in the *doing and having* level of life, you have learned to trust the Creative Process. When you are working at the spiritual level, however, the Creative Process requires more than just the focus and action associated with blind faith. It requires you to take off the blinders and delve into your psyche to determine the *nature* of your thoughts and feelings.

What is the primary attitude, the dominant vibration, the chief feature that has defined you since you were small—the attitude you have unconsciously supported all your life through your affirming choices? What are the attitudes that have quietly directed your choices? In other words, what are those attitudes that make up your being?

Applying what you have learned in working with the Creative Process to the seeking out of the internal obstacles that are separating you from a full awareness of yourself as an unlimited, spiritual being is understanding faith. It is the work involved in changing your being.

Why Blind Faith Is Necessary

The question most people ask is this: *Shouldn't I be using all my creative processes, including those directed toward "doing and having," to delve into my psyche? Wouldn't this help me move more quickly toward understanding who I really am?* It seems that the answer to this question would be a resounding "Yes!" However, as strange as it may sound, using blind faith to *do and have* the things you desire is an important part of your journey. Let me explain why.

The Creative Process is an unchanging and ever-present principle. You use it whether you are aware of it or not. However, it is only when you *consciously* use it to *do and have* and begin to see it work that you learn to **trust it without question**. Once this happens, you may very quickly find yourself turning inward toward the spiritual level of your life. Because of the belief you now have in the Creative Process through blind faith, you are better prepared to delve into your psyche and accomplish positive change. Your focus can now be totally on the work you need to do because you trust the tool you are using.

For a simple comparison, think back to the first time you learned to drive an automobile, particularly if it was a stick-shift. So much of your focus was on the mechanics of trying to operate the clutch with the accelerator and the brake, steering, checking the mirrors, watching traffic, watching your speed, and expecting the worst that driving the car seemed like an impossible task. If someone had asked you that first time to drive in rush hour traffic on the freeway, you would probably have had a heart attack! However, once you learned to drive around the parking lot and on the neighborhood streets without incident, you not only trusted the car, you trusted your ability to use it. Then you were able to actually direct energy to where you were going and enjoy the scenery along the way!

This is why it is necessary for you to focus on the process itself for a while before you start trying to *consciously* use the Creative Process to change your being. Just try to consciously use the Creative Process to *do* something or *have* something. Don't worry about changing your being. You're not ready to tackle rush hour traffic. Give it a little time, and you will be.

Caveat

Do not make the mistake of thinking that once you begin to work at the spiritual level to change your being, you have moved beyond the need for blind faith.

In the *doing and having* level of your life, blind faith is always the best approach. Even if you are now able to work at the spiritual level, it is not necessary to focus on changing your being to manifest a new car, for example. You simply employ the Creative Process that you have learned to consciously use and move toward your goal. If you allow yourself to get caught up in working on negative aspects of your psyche, you will withdraw energy from your worldly goal.

Most of us want to believe that our ability to *do and have* is directly proportional to our "goodness" or our spirituality. This, of course, brings up the dilemma of why some of the wealthiest and most successful people you read about also turn out to be the most devious and egotistical. It doesn't seem to go hand in hand with the commonly accepted ideas put forth about prosperity and spiritual growth, does it?

The truth is that these unsavory individuals appropriately used blind faith in the Creative Process to *have* financial success. They did not waste time worrying about their state of being. They were completely involved in the *doing and having* level of life.

Your spirituality does not determine your ability to *do and have*. It can certainly influence your attitude toward doing and having, but *not* your ability.

As I said in the beginning, there are two levels to your life: a worldly one and a spiritual one. You should always use **blind faith** when working at the worldly level and **understanding faith** when working at the spiritual level. They both have their place.

Magnetic Center: The Spiritual Perspective

Have you ever looked at your life and said, "Is this it? Is this all there is?" Have you come to a place where your success, your knowledge and all that you've accomplished are no longer fulfilling? Do you find yourself constantly wondering if there's more to life than this? Do you wonder what happened to that person who was able to get so excited about life not long ago? Are you wondering why life now feels shallow and meaningless most of the time?

Good for you! I say this because this feeling is not a negative, despite how it feels. It's an opportunity! Why? Because it heralds the fact that you are on the threshold of adding a new dimension to your life. It is the genesis of *magnetic center*.

Impetus Toward Magnetic Center

Many people encounter magnetic center as a result of profound disappointment, such as failure to achieve an important life goal. Sometimes magnetic center is triggered by a feeling that something is missing from your life and you have no idea what it is. That is how I first embraced magnetic center.

A feeling that something was missing was nagging me. I thought perhaps I was losing my faith. So I began going to church every Sunday and at every other opportunity, but this did not appease my growing sense of uneasiness. If it did anything, it increased my feeling of discomfort. I felt I had slipped into an alternate reality. Nothing seemed as it had been anymore. Since then I have discovered that this state of mind is not unusual during this transitional time. Many others have experienced this same dilemma. Are you one of them?

You are created to be a growing, unlimited being, and your *dissatisfaction* is the way that the universe reminds you of this fact. Self-imposed limitations keep you living the futile existence of investing all your energy outward. When you see the contrast between the limitations under which you live and the unlimited potential that *could be*, you experience the beginning influence of magnetic center.

The Part Magnetic Center Plays In Your Life

Magnetic center becomes active when you begin to believe that life has no answers in and of itself. Under the guidance of magnetic center, you begin adjusting your attention. Rather than being focused totally on the outer world and allowing it to guide your judgments, you begin interpreting life and its circumstances from a more internal and intelligent place.

To think like this, you must look beyond the appearance of things and find the invisible source behind them. You can take nothing at face value. Your relationships with people, experiences, and the world at large are used as your means of finding a deeper meaning in life. Finding this deeper meaning causes you to be more discerning about what works and what doesn't.

Possessing magnetic center allows you the spiritual perspective of seeing the relationship between your inner and outer worlds so that you can make the necessary adjustments in what you think and feel. This insight gives you the power to be the victor, not the victim of life because it discards bad ideas and uses only the good. It's good to remember that the contents of your inner world replicate themselves in your world of experiences.

Two Approaches To Life

Developing magnetic center helps you draw a line in the sand by clearly differentiating between two approaches to life.

If you take the first approach to life, you could be described as a person who does your job, pays your bills, keeps your promises, fulfills your contracts, and is an all-around upstanding person in nearly every area of your life. You believe that the values and priorities of the world, or life, are meaningful and fulfill a lasting purpose. We call this person Good Householder #1.

If you take the second approach to life, you could be described as a person who does your job, pays your bills, keeps your promises, fulfills your contracts, and is an all-around upstanding person in nearly every area of your life. We call this person Good Householder #2.

So...what's the difference? The difference is that unlike Good Householder #1, *Good Householder #2 does not believe that the values and priorities of the world, or life, are meaningful and serve any lasting purpose.* The attitude of Good Householder #2 is that of a person who has magnetic center.

Another Benefit Of Magnetic Center

Under the power of magnetic center, you can also see the differences between the influences exerted on you. These influences are called A, B and C influences.

A influences are those exerted on you from life. These influences attempt to convince you that your good lies in the things of life. That's why there are wars and disputes – because one person feels that another is trying to take their good. Crime arises out of the belief that someone else has what should be yours. The fashion industry bases all its marketing on making you believe that the only way you can be happy is to dress and look the way they say is acceptable.

C influences come down to you from the what is called the "conscious circle of humanity." The conscious circle of humanity represents the highest spiritual understanding and ideals that have come from all the advanced souls in the universe. Unfortunately, we do not have the mechanism necessary to receive this information in its highest forms.

B influences are combinations of A and C influences. Since we cannot receive C influences in pure form, they are mixed in with the knowledge of the world in which we live. Consequently, C influences merge with A influences to become B influences. The result of this would be the Gospels and other wisdom teachings.

A person with magnetic center understands the difference between A and C influences. They recognize that the source of their power and their strength cannot be found by pursuing A influences. They recognize that the understanding they seek can be found in the esoteric messages, messages written in a language they can understand, which are found in the B influences. These are the teachings that recognize that you are designed to "be in the world but not of the world." They understand that the flow of energy is from the within to the without. In other words, your happiness comes from within. These teachings stress the creative potential of every individual.

So, Now What?

Possessing magnetic center is like gaining admission to college. You've stepped over the threshold, and now the work begins. In college you establish a major and begin the process of acquiring the knowledge and experience necessary to move into a new level of experience in that field.

This new level of life is no different. Developing magnetic center takes you over the threshold. Now you must decide on your focus, absorb the knowledge and develop the understanding that will allow you to move fully into a new level of experience.

Of course, you can also make the same choices many make in college. You can choose to walk away. Many do. It takes commitment and courage to stay the course. It is up to you. Despite the way it may seem at times, the universe is very kind to us. Sometimes, however, this kindness comes in the form of *tough love*. The basic premise of tough love is that *the best thing you can do to help someone wake up is allow them to take responsibility for the consequences manifesting in their life.*

Developing A Fearless Attitude

If you choose to ignore those haunting questions you have about your life and continue to look to the world, the answers you find will be fleeting or unfulfilling. This will never change until you embrace your potential as a creative being. I hope, however, that the next time you feel overwhelmed by lack or disappointment, you recognize that the universe is trying to open your mind up to embrace your magnetic center.

PERSONALITY: YOUR MEDIUM OF EXCHANGE

Have you ever caught yourself adapting what you say or how you act to win someone else's approval or just to keep from ruffling their feathers? I know you've noticed others' doing it. When that happened, you had a front row seat on how a personality can change to meet the needs of the moment.

Psychology defines personality as "the patterns of behaviors, thoughts, and emotions unique to an individual, and the ways they interact to help or hinder the adjustment of a person to other people and situations." That's quite a mouthful, but what it is saying is this: You are constantly shifting your personality to influence and impress other people, either positively or negatively.

We may describe one person as having a pleasing personality, another as shy, and yet another as outgoing. These attitudes that we identify as their personalities may actually only be one aspect of their personalities. Others can choose to like, dislike, or ignore one or many of the attitudes that make up your personality. However, your personality is not the real you. It is the mask or the "false face" you use to deal with the changing circumstances and people in your world. We live in a world of false people – people who have taken on as their own the attitudes they've seen others use to survive.

Don't get me wrong. Personality is necessary. It is the way in which you interact in this world. There are certain things you learn that help you get along with others and help you make your way in the world. The problem with Personality arises when you no longer understand that it is only the mechanism through which you communicate and interact. The problem worsens as you gradually accept the idea that the answers that you need are out there in the world. That's when you begin to judge yourself by what the world thinks. Your spirit soars or tumbles according to how well the world thinks you're doing. You have turned away from the real YOU.

Developing A Fearless Attitude

You came to this planet of lesson as a seed idea with the sole purpose of developing into a mature spiritual being. In order to do this, you had to take a body and join other spiritual beings who also took physical form. For most of us, this is where the trouble started. Why? Because the "physical you" has to express through a personality, and as I just described, it tends toward misdirection by trying to conform to the expectations of the other personalities making up the world.

Hidden behind your personality is what you "ought to be." Your higher, spiritual nature is the driving force that works behind and through your personality to goad you into a better life. It is the subtle driving force behind your attempts at going beyond what you are and what you are now experiencing.

Your fear of trying something different is an indication that your Personality is looking in the wrong direction for support. You should look within, not without. The more your spiritual nature influences your Personality, the more stable you become. No longer are you that "reed shaking in the wind" mentioned in the Bible. You have developed an inner strength that is unshakable. When the Bible says that "the kingdom of heaven is within you," it means it literally! Your portal is within you.

Make sure you understand that your Personality is NOT a bad thing. It is your essential medium of exchange for developing into a higher state of being and thus changing your life. The only reason your Personality becomes an obstacle for you is that you forget it is not YOU. It is simply a mechanism that the REAL you uses to grow.

Developing A Fearless Attitude

THE IMPACT OF PERSONALITY ON YOUR ESSENCE

First, we need to address the nature of your essence and its connection to your personality. Essence is defined as "a basic trait that defines and establishes the character of something." So *your* essence is the part of you that is real and everlasting — the part that goes with you into your next life experience.

So, when you were born, you were pure essence. You had no attitudes, no beliefs, other than what you brought with you into this life. Unfortunately, one of the elements necessary to survive and interact in the world is the development of personality. It is in the active development of your personality that your essence becomes passive. Your challenge in this life is to once again make essence active by making personality passive. The Bible refers to this by saying, "You must become as a little child."

As mentioned earlier, your success in this life is not determined by how much you acquire or how many worldly goals you achieve. It is determined solely on how well you made your personality — that part of you that thinks from the perspective of worldly values — passive so that you could express from your essence.

Enlightenment?

What does the much sought-after state called Enlightenment have to do with your essence? Well, most people see a direct connection between what they know and enlightenment. As a result, calling oneself "enlightened" has become a badge of honor. The truth is that such a blatant ego trip only gets in the way of your enlightenment. It adds to your personality, not your essence. The truly "enlightened" recognize that it is not a static state, but rather an ongoing process whose beginnings and endings are not so clearly defined.

One thing we do know for sure is that there is a direct connection between the act of making your personality passive and your essence active and the onset of enlightenment. In other words, you should make the effort to grow your essence.

Are You A Good Egg?

Before we can talk about growing your essence, I want to give you a visual for the relationship between your personality and your essence. This relationship can be compared to the relationship between the embryo of an egg and its yolk. Both your essence and the embryo in an egg grow by consuming what is around them.

In an egg, the embryo is surrounded by a yellow yolk, which is in turn surrounded by a clear liquid. All of this is safely contained in a shell. The embryo is the seed idea — the essence — from which the chicken grows. If the egg is kept warm, the embryo begins to grow. It does this by consuming the yolk for its further development into a chicken. If, for any reason, the egg is not kept warm, it stays undeveloped and there is a chance that you might eat it for breakfast with toast and hash browns.

You came into this world psychologically as pure essence — like the embryo inside the egg shell. Through living your life, this pure essence is gradually surrounded by the yolk of personality. Your personality is created through the ideas, values, and priorities, both good and bad, that you learn from experience or accept from others as true. They surround your essence. The more experiences you have that affirm your worldly beliefs, the stronger those beliefs become, and the stronger the influence of your personality on your life.

Can you begin to see how the relationship between your essence and your personality within the shell you call your life are similar to the development of the chicken? The embryo in the egg uses the yolk as nourishment to develop fully. So must your essence consume your personality in order to develop fully. Consequently, as your essence grows, your personality must diminish.

Developing A Fearless Attitude

You're probably wondering: "But what would I do without my personality? This is what I use to deal with my life!" Don't panic. Your personality is not destroyed. It is consumed by a higher, more conscious part of you. While your personality is a good thing, it also contains the values taught to you by the world. Imagine what you would be like if you were without these earthy limitations! What would your life be like if you could see your experiences untainted by the biases you have developed throughout your existence?

Let's go back for a moment to the analogy of the egg. Remember that the embryo only matures to a certain place and then stops without the addition of warmth. Your essence is exactly the same. It only grows to a certain place and then stops if something else is not added from the outside. The hen sitting on the egg provides the warmth the embryo needs to grow. YOU provide the "something else" that your essence needs to grow. This "something else" that you apply to grow your essence is what discovering the power within you is all about.

The "something else" that you add is understanding—understanding of who you really are and your unlimited creative potential. It is the understanding that your essence is your link to your spirituality. It is the "trait that defines and establishes the character" of who you really are. The more you apply the warmth of understanding to your essence, the more you will develop into the conscious spiritual being you were meant to be.

When Jesus, the Master Teacher, said "These things you see me do, you shall do also," he was not speaking of your personality, He was speaking of the essence of you, telling you of the amazing possibilities held within your essence.

◐ Utilize Spiritual Tools

THREE TOOLS FOR A BETTER LIFE

Have you ever wondered why all your hard work never seems to pay off? Why is it some people prosper with little or no effort? The reason is that they understand, consciously or intuitively, how to access the unlimited potential which is available to us all. This unlimited potential consists of everything you can desire, existing first as ideas waiting to manifest in your life. Three tools needed to access them and bring them into expression are *faith, wisdom,* and *love.*

Wait! These are not religious concepts. These are the tools you use to build your life, and we all use them. It is only lack of awareness which causes us to use them improperly. Faith, wisdom, and love are impersonal. They can be used to manifest your greatest dreams, your worst nightmares, and everything in between. The skill with which we use them is up to us.

Our Supreme Affirmative Power

Faith is considered by most people to be a measure of their confidence, whether that confidence is in their concept of God, in some individual, or in an idea. This measure of confidence directly affects our willingness for this person or idea to express in or be a part of our lives. It gives permission. Philosophers describe faith as the "supreme affirmative power." In other words, it is our power to say "yes" to something.

Look around you. What have you said "yes" to in your life? Your social life, the money in your pocket or the bank, the health you are experiencing, and your state of mind exist because you said "yes" to them. You had faith in them. You gave them permission—the power—to exist as they are in your life. If you are perfectly happy with your life, being responsible for it is an easy concept to accept. If, however, you are broke, out of work, miserable in your job, or sick, it is difficult to admit that you gave these ideas, these conditions, permission to express in your life.

The unlimited potential into which we tap includes *all* possibilities, not just what we deem good things. Faith is impersonal. Faith does not care in what you put your confidence. It simply waits for your instructions, just like your car does. Your car doesn't care whether you drive to the store or over a cliff. It simply responds to your direction. The power of faith is your *power of choice!*

How Appropriate Are Our Choices?

How do we learn to make better choices? We learn to use the power of **wisdom**. Instead of unthinkingly saying "yes" to ideas, you develop a mental platform from which you can impartially observe what you think and then discern or *judge its appropriateness*. Your conditioning robs you of your awareness of this tool. Consequently, you continue to do the same things over and over and expect different results. This is the definition of insanity! Overcoming your conditioning is a slow process. It begins by simply being aware that you have put your confidence in conditions not because you used wisdom in choosing them, but because you are conditioned to accept them as your reality.

Suppose you desire prosperity. You have confidence—faith—that it can be yours. You use wisdom to discern that your spending patterns are keeping you from having any money to invest. You recognize that you must use your money differently if you expect your financial conditions to improve. Yet, you still have little money left over to put in savings. Unexpected expenses seem to occur at every turn.

What is wrong? You are not using the power of the final tool to bring your potential into your experiences. This tool is **love**.

Developing A Fearless Attitude

Why Do We Attract Bad Things Into Our Lives?

Although love in the human experience often expresses as feelings, it is actually your *attracting power*. Like the power of faith, it, too, is impersonal. It attracts into your life anything on which you focus your attention. This attention can be focused on having something or on *not* having something. Fighting against something, however, focuses your attention on what you don't want and manifests it in your life. The Universe does not understand qualifiers. It does not understand that you don't want this experience. It only responds to the energy you are investing in your thoughts and feelings about it. So you can see how resistance is indeed *focused attention* and how the use of wisdom can assist you in making better choices about what to invest your energy in!

You can have an affinity for a number of things which would short-circuit your conscious desire for prosperity. You are often comfortable with the familiar. As noted in the earlier example, you may not be able to pay your bills every month or have any money left for other things, but you know how to deal with these conditions. Despite your desire for prosperity, you have developed a relationship with lack, an affinity for it. Therefore, what you attract into your life are situations which create these conditions, in other words, the unexpected expenses.

To Reach Goals, You Need These Tools

These tools are at work when you wonder why you keep finding yourself in abusive relationships—whether personal or business, losing despite all your efforts, or repeating the same negative experiences in any area of your life. It is *also* at work when you find yourself surrounded by loving relationships and winning at every turn!

In goal-setting, you are always instructed to affirm your goals every day and visualize what it will take to achieve them. This creates the necessary mental atmosphere that allows you to say

Developing A Fearless Attitude

"yes" to your desire (**faith**), to discern the best action for accomplishing it (**wisdom**), and to develop an affinity for this new experience, your goal, through this daily ritual (**love**).

Remember these three things:

- Faith, wisdom, and love are impersonal.
- You are the directing force behind all of these tools.
- These tools, these powers, are being used by you at all times whether you are consciously aware of it or not.

SELF-OBSERVATION: A SPIRITUAL DISCIPLINE

Do you self-observe? If you're like most people, you probably answered, "Of course! I'm always aware of how I look, what I'm doing, and the reason I'm doing it!" However, that's not really true. Oh, sure, if you think *back*, you can probably recall those things, but at that moment you were more likely on automatic pilot. We all do it. We have habitual responses to most things in life. In other words, habitual actions and attitudes kick in before we have time to think through a suitable response.

Of course, I'm not really being fair because you probably think that self-observation is about monitoring yourself and then making judgments about your actions. The good news is that it is about NOT making judgments about your actions!

The self-observation I am talking about is a spiritual discipline. It is the act of separating yourself into two parts — the Observer and the Observed. The Observer is the part of you that watches the parade of thoughts and feelings as they pass through your mind without criticism or judgment. It makes you aware of your inconsistencies. It does this by noticing your performance as you adapt what you think, do, and say to successfully maneuver your way through your daily interactions without experiencing too much upheaval.

For instance, have you ever been saying something to someone and heard that voice within you saying, "You don't believe a word you're saying." You can tell if the voice is your Observer *if* you don't feel guilty about it or judge yourself in any way. Remember that self-observation **MUST** be done *without criticism* and *without judgment*. To self-observe you must be in a mental space where you are an onlooker, not a participant.

Without self-observation, you can never accomplish the most important thing you came to this planet to do as a spiritual being —

raise your consciousness. Self-observation lets you glimpse the threshold between the life of a machine and that of an awakening being. Without self-observation, you can be a smashing success in the eyes of the world and be a failure in the most important thing you can do as a spiritual being having a human experience.

The act of observing separates. You cannot observe something if it's up close and personal. So, the act of observing a negative thought or feeling separates you from it. It gives you the opportunity to stop fueling the negativity! When this happens, the ability of the negativity to influence your life is lessened.

Self observation, as painful as it can sometimes be, continually makes you aware that you are quite often in a deep sleep, responding to circumstances not as a thinking being, but rather as a machine. Self-observation makes you aware of issues, ideas, and feelings that are cutting you off from your higher good. You cannot experience a higher consciousness unless you're willing to change, that is, to let go of the consciousness in which you're now living!

No one likes the idea that they are like a machine. I don't either. Unfortunately, our conditioning causes us to live the life of one. Conditioning is a powerful influence in everyone's life. Much of our conditioning is caused by our associations with people and our tendency to pattern ourselves after them. Most of the limiting thoughts and negative feelings that inhibit our lives were not conscious choices. We started borrowing them from the people around us when we were quite small. Out of force of habit, we continue to accept what others say about us as true.

Just remember! The greatest power conditioning has to cut you off from a better life is your being unaware that it exists. Living in the illusion that you are a thinking being, who is always responding to life's circumstances creatively, is what supports the status quo. For this reason you can live your life in a state of deep sleep and, for all practical purposes, be okay. Of course, as I said before, when you persist in living the life of a machine, you lose the opportunity to increase your consciousness.

Why is this so important, besides the fact that it is what you came here to do? You are a creative being. It is your birthright. Creativity is synonymous with change, with growth, with expansion. Creativity cannot stand still. If you want to reach your highest potential, you can't either, and self-observation is the key that will open that door to the expansion of your being.

Developing A Fearless Attitude

SELF-REMEMBERING: DISENGAGING FROM YOUR ROLES

Do you remember the actor/comedian Jonathan Winters? He was my favorite. He had an hilarious routine where he would pluck a hat out of a trunk and then become the character represented by that hat. Years later I read that Mr. Winters was having personal problems because he couldn't seem to separate his real self from all the characters he created.

We are in the same boat as Jonathan Winters. All the subpersonalities within us, which I will discuss in greater detail in the Healing section of this book, are just like the characters Winters took on with every change of his hat. When we put on the hat of some subpersonality that we created to deal with certain situations in our lives, we fit ourselves into the role, experiencing the attitudes appropriate to that "hat." We become like the actor because we have forgotten we are playing a role.

So, where does self-remembering come into all of this? Self-remembering is like when the actor, who is entirely absorbed by the part he is playing, suddenly remembers that he is just acting out a part. Until he had that moment of clarity, he was asleep or unaware of his true reality.

How do you manage to self-remember? Well, first of all, just realizing that you ARE mechanical is a step in the right direction. Self-observation makes it possible for you to become a spectator of your own actions and moves you closer to being able to self-remember so that you can become a conscious creator of your life.

Self-Remembering Is The Act Of Disengaging.

What is involved? You remove yourself from your negative emotions. You release all attitudes. You simply are. Sounds simple, but it is definitely not! The biggest enemy of self-remembering is the tendency to identify—that is, to invest your sense of who you are into the world of conditions surrounding you.

If you could, even for a moment, empty yourself of all attitudes, regrets, petty misgivings, jealousies, and a multitude of other thoughts and feelings and become nobody, you would be practicing self-remembering. In the Bible this act is called *"going into the closet."*

Self-Remembering Is The Act Of Taking Time To Remember Who You Really Are.

The words "I am a spiritual being having a human experience" roll off our tongues without much thought being given to the reality of the statement. If we really believed that we are primarily spiritual beings, we would put more energy into focusing inward, not outward. We would realize that our real Source is within, not without.

Self Remembering Is Taking The Time To Reconnect With Source Energy.

Over the years I have found it to be as difficult as it is beneficial. Focusing on nothing is difficult when all the concerns of the day are vying for your attention. Here is a good exercise that I have used to keep myself humble and to strengthen my ability to self-remember by thinking about nothing.

Find a watch or a clock that has a second hand. See how long you can keep your attention on the second hand without being distracted. If you can keep your attention on the second hand without even the slightest distraction (*no* thoughts except for watching the second hand), for 30 seconds, my hat is off to you! You are ready!

When I practice self-remembering, I disengage myself from the world by saying mantras like, "I am not these thoughts ... I am not this body ... I am using this body to express in this world ... I am not these feelings ... I am a spiritual being having a physical experience ... I am a spiritual being and have come into this experience free of worldly attachments and limitations."

Developing A Fearless Attitude

Try it. It takes time to experience a moment (yes, I said a moment) of self-remembering. Most of us hardly ever experience more than a few moments of self-remembering at a time because the pull of the world is so strong. However, those moments make such a difference in our perspective of life that it is incredible!

Don't be surprised if after you self-remember, you start to understand what is meant by "hiding your light under a basket."

THE NINE BASIC STEPS OF MEDITATION

Peace of mind and clarity of thought are important for anyone. So many things run through your mind in the course of the day that you need to be able to center yourself. Meditation is the tool for achieving this. Take time to practice the steps below, and you will be amazed by how creative you become!

So, okay, you're going to meditate... Piece of cake! After all, how hard can it be? All you need to do is sit down and close your eyes and relax, right? Wrong! If this were true, everyone who ever attempted meditation would have mastered it, and you know that is just not the case. The old axiom about there being no such thing as a free lunch is something you might want to remember when you begin the process of learning to meditate.

When you go through the following, realize that your body is like a spoiled child and will resist your attempts to discipline it. Consistency is one of the keys for becoming proficient in meditation. So, **make a commitment to practice daily for at least 21 days**, which is the time necessary to initiate change.

What we present below is not the only way to meditate. It is simply the easiest way to learn. A walking meditation can occur for you as you practice the Presence and believe fully in God as your Source.

Step One: **FIND A QUIET PLACE** where you will not be disturbed for 20 or 30 minutes. Shut the phone off so that the ring will not disturb you while you practice. In these beginning days, make sure that you are not in an environment where electrical fans, radios, or machines are running. Later, when you have a degree of mastery, you will learn to use background noise as a means of deepening your meditative experience.

Step Two: **FIND A COMFORTABLE PLACE** to sit down or lie down. Be aware that in the initial stages, you may have a tendency to fall asleep. Therefore, sitting upright may be more practical than lying down. When you sit, place both feet flat on the floor. It will make you feel more composed and determined about your efforts. As a side note, if you should fall asleep, you probably needed the rest. When you wake up, try again. There are no penalties for "do overs."

Step Three: After being seated, decide how to **POSITION YOUR BODY**, that is, where you want to place your hands and arms. This could be in your lap or on the arms of your chair. You may need to experiment a little to find out just where they feel most comfortable. At first it may seem awkward no matter where you put them.

Step Four: Now that you are seated, **CLOSE YOUR EYES**. Because your attention is still behind your eyelids, you may see tiny points of light, squiggles, or variations of light. After you move through the rest of the steps, you will find that your awareness will automatically shift to a place on your forehead just above and between your eyes. This place is called the third eye or the seat of the imagination.

Step Five: Slowly and easily **TAKE FULL BREATHS**. As you do, feel the flow of air as it goes down into your lungs and back out again. If you are breathing properly, your stomach should seem to swell and your chest will move very little because you are using your diaphragm. The most efficient muscle of breathing, the diaphragm is located at the base of the lungs. Your abdominal muscles help move the diaphragm and give you more power to empty your lungs. Practice this at least 10 times.

Step Six: **RELAX THE BODY** by using the following exercises.

Developing A Fearless Attitude

1) Press the toes of your right foot firmly down against the floor until you feel tension in the entire foot. Do this for the count of 10. Then relax. You may feel an increase in warmth, a slight tingle, or the foot may just seem to feel larger.

2) Do the same exercise with the right foot again. Now the difference in feeling between the right foot and the left foot gives you the contrast you need to tell the difference between a body part that is experiencing a degree of relaxation and one that is still in a state of tension.

3) Perform the same exercise with the left foot. Now both feet are in a state of relaxation.

4) Your challenge now is to allow this feeling of relaxation to flow upward into the rest of your body. You do this by tensing each body part, holding the tension for a few seconds, and then letting go. Allow this feeling of warmth (relaxation) to flow slowly up through your ankles, lower legs, knees, thighs, lower body, chest, arms, neck, face and scalp. Any place you especially feel tension, tense that body part again and then let go.

Pay close attention to the muscles in your face. Relax the lips. Allow the tongue to lie loosely in the floor of the mouth. Keep the jaw relaxed. Do not let your teeth close tightly. A good approach for relaxing all the face muscles is to make the most ferocious monster face you can muster and then relax.

Step Seven: **QUIET THE BRAIN**. Your random patterns of thought are one of the greatest enemies of meditation, and it takes an heroic effort to bring them under control. The good news is that your focus on the process required in relaxation has already given you some degree of control.

However, to fully benefit from meditation, you have to bore your brain into submission! You do this by taking a word or phrase, called a mantra, and saying it over and over. A mantra can be a word such as "Love" or a phrase such as "God and I are One." If you catch your thoughts wandering to the obligations you have or the grocery list, bring them back to your mantra. Getting your brain under control is also like retraining a spoiled child. It resists your efforts, but eventually, your consistency and commitment to the process will bring it under control.

Step Eight: **LISTEN**. This is not about hearing words. It is more about the feelings or state of mind you experience. You may suddenly experience a knowing about questions you were struggling with earlier or the direction you need to take becomes clearer.

Step Nine: **SELF-REMEMBER**. This step comes with practice. You find yourself connecting with the oneness that exists between you and God, between you and others, between you and the Universe. The illusions that are governing your life start to break down.

Avoid Mind Candy

Do you know what mind candy is? Then let me explain.

Candy tastes good for the time it is in your mouth, but it soon dissolves and is gone. It contains no real lasting value, requires nothing from the person eating it, and in terms of physical health does more harm than good. Regardless, people seek it out time after time because of the sugar high and immediate gratification.

In the same way, many people read and listen to self-improvement books and tapes, looking for the high they get from them. It's stimulating and exciting to listen to the ideas and imagine the wonderful changes that just might happen. However, change does not happen like magic. It takes ***intent, work, and consistency.***

So what they hear or read has no lasting value because they only *imagine* that they are changing. They become mind candy junkies who live off the parade of seminars, books, and tapes, looking for the high, the immediate stimulation and gratification of the senses.

Because people delude themselves into thinking that mind candy is growing their understanding, it actually decays their ability ***to use the discipline necessary for spiritual growth*** and in the end does more harm than good.

That sounds a bit harsh, doesn't it? But when you look at all the millions of self-help books, recordings, and other things sold each year and ask how much real improvement you see around you, you have to admit—there could be a point here.

How Can This Benefit You?

Be aware of the temptation to indulge in **mind candy**. Take the time to work with new knowledge and your spiritual tools until you can see that a change has occurred in your life. Consistently doing the work necessary is what changes your life forever.

HEALING

Whenever you have a life goal, you know WHAT you want, and of course, you know WHERE you are, but... *how do you get from here to there & survive the journey?*

That's really the question, isn't it? I'm sure you often find yourself overwhelmed with the demands of having to make all the decisions and then carry them out as well. At the end of the day, you find yourself wondering if you'll have enough strength to stay the course.

Unfortunately, our life goals often drain the energy we should be investing in our spiritual life, our relationships, and our family if we are going to maintain balance in our lives. As a result, these areas start to deteriorate. We sometimes refuse to even take time for ourselves.

Were these risks ones that you considered when you so diligently prepared your business plan or set a course toward your goal? Probably not! Rest assured. It's not necessary to pay such a heavy price to see your dreams come true!

In our race toward success, a lack of balance often leads to dis-ease, which manifests in many different ways. Our plan, our foundation, for success must include the healing of our inner world. After all, it is who we are inside that determines the quality and longevity of our desired success.

◐ Break Old Patterns

DOES IT FEEL LIKE YOU'RE IN A RUT?

Are you in a rut? If you take a minute to look up the word *rut*, you will see it defined as a "fixed, dull, and unpromising way of life." If I could actually take a survey of the private thoughts of everyone on this planet, I dare to say that I would discover the vast majority feel that their lives, though they may look exciting to others, could be described as fixed, dull, or unpromising. Most of us would never admit this if asked by another, of course. Such a disclosure subjects us to the possibility of being considered a failure. The ideal concept of success, at least in the United States, requires that your life be dynamic, exciting, and full of promise.

You may be successful in terms of accomplishments, money, family, or whatever and still feel that your life is unpromising or dull. This creates a conundrum. *How can I truly be successful, despite the outer evidence, if my life is not dynamic, exciting, and full of promise to me?*

The Letdown

Most people discover when they achieve a major goal in their lives, particularly related to careers or family, that it never has the long-lasting, exhilarating effect they imagined it would. It's not long before they feel an emptiness, a longing for the excitement they experienced on the climb toward their earlier goal.

The operative word here is *climb*. As we work hard to accomplish a goal, we are literally **climbing out of one level of understanding into another**. For example: Whether we actually succeed in achieving our goal of a college degree, a high-powered job, or losing sixty pounds, doesn't mean we have failed because we no longer have the same perspective we had before we began moving toward the goal.

The problems arise when we settle in, making ourselves comfortable, when we rest on our laurels, whether in our career, family, or personal lives, and consequently expect that one, concentrated, perhaps superhuman, effort from our past to be the culminant, to be the highest point of our striving. When we do this, we will find ourselves in a **RUT**—a rut where we will sit and bemoan the absence of all the accolades and happiness we thought would be ours when we reached this particular plateau.

Why are we so often afraid to move from this path of resting on our laurels? Is it because it's familiar? Or is it because we no longer trust ourselves to choose a path? After all, we chose this one, and it doesn't feel nearly as good as we thought it would. The answer to this question can be either of these attitudes. However, we may also remain in our familiar rut because we are unwilling to look at our life in terms of change. We say to ourselves: *It is what it is, and there's nothing to be done about it!*

How many times have you heard your parents or someone else say, "You made your bed, now lie in it"? This old adage has a kernel of truth in it. *We did make our own beds.* However, we do not have to lie in this bed *forever!* As with many familiar bits of wisdom, the true value of it has been corrupted by limited thinking—thinking that is resistant to change.

The Reaction

So what do people do when they find themselves feeling empty or bored? Well, some of us convince ourselves that the cause of our discontent is simply a failure to invest enough energy. So, we become workaholics or develop addictions to whatever endeavor represents our success. This investment, as I mentioned earlier, quite often comes at the expense of some other area in our lives. For example, workaholics often neglect their families in terms of quality time spent with them.

Developing A Fearless Attitude

The Solution

There is a solution which does not require us to steal from one area of our lives to service another. To access it may require you to change your *perspective* of life, however. If you pigeon-hole the aspects of your life, making it difficult to see the causal thread connecting them, you will definitely have to re-assess your thinking to utilize this information at its fullest.

The causal thread connecting every part of your life experience is **YOU**. Your belief system, your attitudes, whatever you want to call it, determines the experiences that you have. If you insist on blaming others for your experiences or holding on to the idea that life is victimizing you, climbing out of your rut will be very difficult, perhaps even impossible.

If you *are* ready for a dynamic, exciting, and promising life and are willing to invest your energy judiciously by working to develop a *fearless attitude* toward life, I can promise you that you will develop new strategies for *targeting your potential* that will rise above a particular job, a particular experience, or even a particular relationship. Happiness can change from being an experience that depends on outer conditions to become the way you view the whole experience of living.

The Conundrum

But what about the conundrum: *How can I truly be successful, despite the outer evidence, if my life is not dynamic, exciting, and full of promise to me?*

The conundrum exists because success is a completely subjective term. My answer to that question depends on how I measure success and the choices I make about it. The same is true for you. Therefore, you are left with questions you must ask yourself.

- If I consider success to be possessions or position, will acquisition of more revitalize my life? Will I have to keep adding to my inventory like a junkie to feel alive? Will I ever really feel successful?

- If I measure success by my personal growth, do I understand the reasons my life feels unpromising or dull? Do I understand my culpability, and am I willing to risk another change?

Your answers to these questions and others will determine the choices you make in your life. They will influence whether you choose to climb out of the rut you are in or not.

Even if you know how important personal growth is, you can still be in a rut. Remember that old expression that speaks of "ten years of experience or one year of experience ten times?" Personal growth is hard work, and sometimes we decide we are just not up to it. This is when we become comfortable with the level of understanding we've already achieved, and this is where we choose to live our lives year after year.

A Word of Warning

Just a word of warning – Climbing out of your rut can be a dangerous undertaking. You must have focus and dedication. You must develop the discipline and strength required to withstand the storms that can accompany the change in prevailing winds. You must never look behind you. Always keep your focus on where you want to go. Stay alert.

Remember: You'll confront many treacherous situations, but the choices you make are up to you. If you fall, get up. Keep going. Those who give up simply die or tumble backwards into the rut from which they came.

Finally, when you think you've reached the top, don't be fooled. You can rest for a while, but you must go on *or* that level place will simply become another rut.

Developing A Fearless Attitude

If you are truly committed to creating a new life for yourself, I would suggest listening to our award-winning, 5 CD audio book: *It's Your Move! Transform Your Dreams From Wishful Thinking To Reality.* These 5 CDs can change your perspective and your world.

Is Procrastination Your Bedfellow?

"We have left undone those things which we ought to have done."
                                        - The Book Of Common Prayer

Stop right now and make a list of all the things you've been putting off in regard to your business or your life in general. [Pause]

Well, now that you have that list on paper [or at least in your head], what would you say is the reason that you haven't been willing to tackle these issues? Is it procrastination? Or is it laziness, fear of success, or because you feel you have too much to do?

You probably answered yes to at least one of these. However, the truth is: procrastination is not a cause but is rather a result of attitudes and conditions. Let's list some of the causes of procrastination:

- you're afraid of success
- your goals are unclear
- you don't know how to approach a problem
- health challenges
- poor self-image
- lack of the necessary learning to handle the issue
- lack of organization
- negativity
- shyness

How often have you allowed one of these attitudes to convince you not to do something?

The Essential Step

The essential step in overcoming procrastination is not focusing on the procrastination. Instead, **focus on one of the things on your list**, one of the things you've been putting off. Determine what is keeping you from doing the task.

Be honest. Don't make excuses. Don't blame others. If it's a task that needs to be done, then your goal is to figure out how to accomplish it.

Write out a list of what it will take to accomplish this task. This step serves to create order, and it jump-starts your creative juices.

For some, writing out a list is almost impossible. An alternative is to inspire your process by picking out something to do related to the task and do it. Then do another thing related to the task. Eventually, you will have enough elements of the task completed that you will be inspired to complete it.

Article writing is an important task for entrepreneurs in this internet age because it is a large part of their marketing. However, it often falls prey to procrastination and becomes a huge obstacle for many. Some think you have to know what you're going to say before you start or at least have an outline. Consequently, they never manage to get articles written.

You don't have to do either. You should decide on a topic. Then sit down at your computer and start writing from your heart. Take your time. Allow yourself to see what you've written out and imagine where your thought processes should go from there. The next thing you know - you'll have an article written!

Creating a list is just a first step in overcoming procrastination, but it is an important one. It forces you to turn your attention away from the causes of your procrastination. Then it centers your focus on the steps necessary to complete your task.

Don't expect this to always be a pleasant exercise. The attitudes and conditions that caused you to procrastinate will continue to voice their opinions in your head. It is up to you whether you direct your attention to their whining or instead keep a clear eye on the task at hand. It is up to you to monitor your reactions if you really want to succeed in whatever you choose to undertake

Developing A Fearless Attitude

DO YOU DETOUR RATHER THAN CHANGE?

Are you open to change? Are you willing to try a different path than the one you've been on? If you answered yes to these questions, I have to ask, "How resistant are you to input from outside yourself?" Do you try to maintain your attitude about yourself, no matter how denigrating it may be, rather than open yourself up to new ideas or ways of doing things?

You may think I am only talking about internal attitudes or your self-image. Of course, your attitude toward yourself is at the core of it, but how do you really know what that attitude is except through how you interact with the world around you? For instance, how about when someone is trying to instruct you about a computer program or trying to logically explain why something works the way it does? Do you insist on holding tight to your feelings that you don't understand computers or refuse to abandon your old perspectives rather than explore a view that may be more productive?

This happens quite often in counseling sessions. Even in trying to get a client to move from point A to point B, a very short distance with no seeming obstacles in sight, the path for the client can often detour by focusing on C, D, E, F, and so on, which are all points that really have no relevance to the ideas in points A and B. However, the client presents them as what they consider valid reasons for being unable to make the short trip of accepting that B logically follows A. Sound convoluted? That's because it is.

Let me give you a simple example. Let us say you were trying to show a person how to do a straightforward operation in Microsoft Word, such as copying from one document and pasting in another, which is simply a rote exercise. Highlight targeted text, hit CTRL-C on the keyboard, click on second document, place cursor where you want the copied text, hit CTRL-V on the keyboard. Done. You would not be expecting to hear the words, "I don't understand because I don't know what everything is called on the computer." Then when you explain that they only need to understand those things related to this operation to accomplish this task, another equally creative reason why they can't do it emerges.

The truth is that these are excuses. They are excuses that mask a number of different internal issues. One could be a fear of relinquishing the status quo. One could be a lack of belief in one's abilities. Another could be the fear of failure or resistance to accepting instruction. There are probably many other possible causes, but they all have one thing in common: they throw up obstacles in the path toward better experiences in your life.

Stop making excuses and focusing on what you think you can't do, and start figuring out how to do what you need to do. In other words, don't look over your shoulder to the past; look ahead to what you want to experience; and start doing something about it in the Now. Of course, we learn from our past, but there's a big difference between learning from the past and living in it.

Developing A Fearless Attitude

PERFECTIONISM IS HIGHLY OVER-RATED!

This is for all those perfectionists out there. We want to think that perfectionism is about having a high degree of excellence. Not true! It is actually about fear. That's right ... FEAR.

Perfectionists are not able to separate their self-worth from their work. Any flaws in their work are considered measurements of their personal worth. So they try to pinpoint all the details about a project and consider all the possibilities for error [which, by the way, is impossible] because they take it personally if anything goes wrong or is not as good as someone else's. That is the fear of rejection. It is the fear that your flaws will be revealed for all the world to see.

The truth is that no one actually expects you to be perfect. Your intent is more important than the millions of details with which you manage to paralyze yourself. If you will allow yourself to do a *good* job, aware that you can make adjustments if they are needed, wondrous things will occur.

- Your stress level will reduce.
- You will be surprised to discover that you don't make as many mistakes as you thought you would.
- Plus, you will realize that some of those things that stared back at you so glaringly in the past were actually quite unimportant to anyone but you.

Relax! The tension you create by striving to be perfect cuts you off from the flow of well-being. So despite your efforts to be perfect, you can never achieve as high a standard of excellence as you will achieve when you are calm, centered, and at peace with yourself.

My Personal Experience

As a recovering perfectionist, I can remember times in high school—in the days of typewriters—when I would re-do a term paper from start to finish because there was a single typo! How ridiculous is that? When I started working, I often worked later than I should have because I spent so much time reviewing my work.

What was I afraid would happen? I was obviously investing a great deal of energy to ward off something! Strangely enough, I don't remember actually putting my feelings about it into words. Of course, if anyone asked, I always chanted my mantra about my desire to do excellent work.

Now that I am much older and find myself being more particular about where I invest my energies, I realize that all that craziness was based on the fear at that time that I wasn't quite good enough. My question now is: *Good enough for whom?*

So now when I experience déjà vu watching some younger person driving themselves over the edge worrying about details that no one will ever notice but them, I try to reach out and touch them. All I can think about is how much valuable time they waste fretting over the small stuff!

You Are Absolutely Good Enough

If you want to spend a lot of your life being unhappy, try to live up to the images that television, magazines, the movies, and your peers say are acceptable. To the world of sleeping people, who are driven by vanity and pride and buy into this insanity, it makes perfect sense because they never connect their unhappiness with their failure to live up to someone else's standards.

To the person who is waking up to the futility of making comparisons, this would seem insane. At the very least, it should make you angry when the world holds up a picture and says, "If you want our approval, this is what you need to look like."

I went to a high school reunion with my spouse, and the last thing on anyone's mind was how they looked. One of the men said he was happy if he woke up on the right side of the dirt. Gruesome thought, but it made a point. Time is the great equalizer. Even if you happen to match what the world considers as beautiful right now, it is a short-lived accomplishment.

So sure, as a human being, you're taught to determine your progress by comparing yourself to others, but what about your progress as a spiritual being? You cannot make comparisons between your level of spiritual understanding and someone else's. It's like comparing apples and oranges. We each have our own unique path, our own unique issues to overcome.

The bottom line is: You came here to learn through your experiences and to develop a spiritual perspective—not to look good in the eyes of the world.

I know you're familiar with the scripture that says a person should be "in the world but not of the world." You are *not* meant to use the world's values to judge yourself. You are meant to discover the power *within you* so that you can live a more prosperous and joy-filled life by knowing that you are absolutely good enough!

Developing A Fearless Attitude

DENIAL AND THE DANCE OF CHAOS

The Dance of Chaos

> Around and around we dance the dance;
> Back and forth in turn we play the game,
> thinking we're winning out over chance
> by keeping things insanely the same.
>
> A moment of clarity perchance arrives,
> but the chaos around us sweeps it away,
> and even that which we see with our own eyes
> can no longer save us. We have lost our way.
>
> Is there hope for one among us whose gallant
> desire is to change the cycles of her life,
> to renew feelings for herself, her talents?
> Yes, there is hope, but it is not without strife.
>
> To change my life, its path and momentum,
> choices must be made, and painful honesty
> must always prevail; Otherwise, to become
> a whole person is only a fantasy.
>
> Making the decision to change is not change;
> It's only the first step along the way.
> My task is to remain alert, for a wide range
> of obstacles can occur to block the way.
>
> I'm not one; I'm many personalities,
> an idea which eludes me so easily.
> I focus on my problems, thinking I see
> who I am, and what it is I want to be.
>
> But, the part of me that's been in charge so long
> is very clever and has more than one face,
> likes its power over me, and sees no wrong
> in whatever it does to maintain its place.

Developing A Fearless Attitude

If I am to rise above my world today,
I have to stay focused on my goal,
not dropping my guard or letting my mind stray
to things which put me back into an old role.

The thinking that got me where I was before
tricks me into thinking things are better now.
I decide I don't need my goals anymore
for I can choose what I will and won't allow.

However, patiently waiting in the wings,
eager to sabotage, are the incumbents.
To my life-changing decisions, their strength brings
resistance, thoughts, emotions—all so intense!

With persistence, I break down my defenses.
Through the struggle, even when I reminisce,
I see hurt, anger, love, all my pretenses,
and know the answer has to be synthesis.

But which ones do I throw away if indeed
there lies within the deepest hurt or anger
a kernel of purity encased in needs,
needs which became distorted from what they were?

Self-discovery will bring both joy and pain
as I untangle my life's choices, making
it seem like familiar chaos once again
when the hardened walls within begin cracking.

A moment of clarity again arrives,
but the chaos no longer sweeps it away;
and even that which I see with my own eyes
is no longer clouded. I have found my way!

©1995 Dannye Williamsen

Why Chaos?

The meaning of the word *chaos* began as a "formless void." Later it took on the more active meaning of "utter confusion." Confusion is the "state of mixing up the mind, mixing up ideas." This jumbling of concepts distracts us from rational thinking because rational thinking requires order.

Why would we desire a state of chaos in our lives? Why would we want to be confused? This is a primordial question in Man's search for psychological well-being. To address this, we should first explore the idea of the ego.

The ego has received much press in the last two centuries. Freud's view of the ego was as the seat of a person's instincts for self-preservation. In other words, an important job of the ego is to make sure that the self-gratification tendencies of the id, another agency of the mind as depicted in Freud's structural model, do not destroy the individual. The ego is the mediator between our baser instincts and the real world.

According to this model, the ego develops through a process of mental conflict, i.e., conflict between the instinctual desires of the id and what the ego can allow if it is to fit into an external reality in a manner it considers functional. One of the ways in which the ego accomplishes this is through the use of defense mechanisms. This is a term we have all heard many times. These are mechanisms we use to defend our Selves against external realities and our own mental contradictions. This defense can set the stage for even more inner conflicts and confusion, which trigger yet other mechanisms for personal survival.

The Mechanism of Denial

A defense mechanism which is familiar to most of us in this modern age is *denial*. Denial is a motivated method of blocking something painful from our conscious awareness. Of course, denial is an unconscious act. Its unconscious nature and the complexity of our personalities contribute to the Dance of Chaos. Because we are unaware of what we are blocking and why, we float across the floor from one state of mind to another—one dance partner to another.

Every partner has a different step, a different rhythm. It keeps us in a constant state of confusion—unable to think rationally, until finally we simply give in to the madness. We refuse to think about it, allowing ourselves to be jostled from one experience to another, all the while denying that our lives are in chaos! We have no clear direction except to maintain the familiar chaos. Most of you reading this will immediately object to the idea that your life is in chaos. After all, you have a job, maybe even one you enjoy, perhaps a spouse and children. Your life is all it is supposed to be. Or is it?

Denial is a mechanism we use when we are afraid to examine something too closely, afraid of what we will find. If we slow down long enough to look at our lives, will we find that we're not really happy? That we are bored? That we're doing the very things we said we would never do?

Denial Is Not Confined To Individuals

Denial keeps us where we are. A few years back I moved to a small town and attempted to integrate into some local civic clubs for women. I wanted to be involved, but I found that involvement did not include new things or new ways of doing things. Suggestions were met with the statement—"That's the way it has always been done!" This was mind-boggling for me, not to mention frustrating.

No matter how carefully I tried to approach them with new ideas or projects, I met tremendous resistance. It either erupted in my face or less obviously later by those who failed to help with the project. I tried very hard to continue but finally came to the following realization.

Developing A Fearless Attitude

A group has the same structural psychology as an individual. The many persons with their respective attitudes and needs parallel the many subpersonalities which make up what we call the Self. Each is vying for attention, but the majority attitude or state of mind controls the consciousness of that group.

In my example, the group was in a state of denial. They had been doing the same things for fifty years or more. Nothing much had changed. Their participation in the activities of the chapter and the national and state organizations were perfunctory. Their main reason for meeting was social—conversation and food. However, their denial of this attitude demanded a strict adherence to the "rules" by them. Why? Because it allowed them to fool themselves into thinking they represented a viable organization, one capable of growing.

When I entered the picture and began to make suggestions which required change or initiation of a new activity, I was unwittingly forcing them to examine the status quo, forcing them to examine their lack of goals, their lack of direction. This was in direct conflict with the state of denial which existed in this group.

I discovered that, most of all, they believed giving in to change would be an indictment of everything they had been doing up to that point. This was the insurmountable obstacle for me. I remained friends with one of the women after I moved away, and I was struck by the gossip which I heard periodically. It was like listening to the same tape over and over. The same arguments between the same people. The same disputes over the same issues. On and on. Denial keeps us where we are.

"Making the decision to change is not change; | It's only the first step along the way. | Our task is to remain alert, for a wide range | Of obstacles can occur to block the way." [The Dance of Chaos]

Representing an "attitude of change" within that group, I did not have enough energy or commitment to sustain the effort against the resistance. Consequently, I allowed myself to fall by the wayside. I gave up the fight. This can happen to each of us on an individual level.

The part of you that desires change will be challenging your present life. It will require you to **examine the who, what, where, why, and how of your life**. To change, you will have to let go of some of your old attitudes. You will need to delve into your thoughts and discover why you fear this change, why it is so hard. Change requires constant energy input. Without it, the strength of the incumbent attitudes will win out.

How Do You Embrace Change?

This Dance of Chaos—moving from one thought to another, one emotion to another, with no purpose, no direction beyond completion of some external task—defines the lives of so many people. It doesn't have to. You can embrace change.

What exactly does change mean? Does it mean change for the sake of change? Some people change jobs, relationships, or towns constantly, seeking a better experience. Usually it doesn't change anything that matters. This is because change or personal growth does not come from external circumstances. It is the result of a change of attitude, a change of perspective on your life. It means letting go of the idea that Life is fate, that Life determines what you experience. It means not giving into the madness.

Looking For The Potential

You are the creator of your life. Are you a "half-full glass" kind of person or a "half-empty glass" person? This old expression simply points out that *we* make the choice on how we view our experiences. Do we see potential or loss?

Truthfully, there is always potential in any experience. The potential may not be found in the physical experience. It may instead involve what we *learned* from that experience. Either way, we can

Developing A Fearless Attitude

choose to see the potential or to focus our energy on what we perceive as lost or negative.

The choice may not be a conscious choice. More often than not, this is the case. We create our experience by default. We allow whatever is in our programming to choose. This is definitely true when we live in a state of denial. We make constant, unconscious choices, and those choices always support our delusions. They never challenge them. If we see ourselves as unattractive, we will interpret every compliment from that view—for example, concluding that the other person was just trying to be nice! Or if the compliment is too contradictory to what we believe, we will ignore it altogether.

If a part of you, what I call a subpersonality, desires personal growth, it will always run up against resistance. However, your conscious effort to notice this part of yourself and honor its needs will eventually crack some of the hardened walls of resistance within you. As I said earlier, in my actions to effect change in the outer world with the women's group, I was not dedicated enough to the effort as a club member to accomplish change. If I had remained and stood firm, eventually change would have been inevitable. The same is true for each of us in our inner worlds

Throw Away Your Dancing Shoes!

You must continue your efforts for personal growth regardless of what you see in your lives at present. Believe in yourself enough to be patient. Throw away your dancing shoes! You are going to need climbing boots. The climb is hard work. Sometimes it will feel like Mt. Everest instead of a simple rut, but focus, determination, and planning will bring you success.

BOOMERANG EFFECT KEEPS YOU RUNNING IN PLACE

Nothing seems to change! Every year it's just more of the same. I've studied the books, gone to the classes, practiced the 3-step, 7-step, and 12-step programs for transforming my life, and I can't understand why things haven't really changed.

Do you feel this way? Well, don't despair. There is a simple explanation. You haven't yet built the necessary internal foundation to support the change you desire. The failure to build a proper foundation executes what we call a boomerang effect where, with frightening speed, you find yourself once again experiencing the same type of limiting relationships, jobs, etc.

The work necessary to build this foundation often focuses on areas so mundane and remote from what you associate with spiritual or personal growth that you never make a connection between these areas and the experiences you seek to change. While the answer to why nothing seems to change is simple, the **process itself** is not easy.

Your conditioning keeps you thinking and doing the same things over and over. You think you are making choices, but those choices are being made by habit. Sounds incredible, but it's true.

- If a person was really thinking, would she get out of one abusive relationship and enter another?
- Would a person move from job to job in search of the perfect situation and encounter instead the same negative experiences as before **without** considering that he is the only common variable?
- Would a person who couldn't stand their domineering father or their whining mother partner with someone just like their parent?

Of course not! To shake yourself loose from some of your conditioning so that you can effect permanent change, you have to begin the **process of** *waking up.*

Developing A Fearless Attitude

Waking Up to Change

Change requires your creative participation. As with any job, you have to learn the basic rules; then you need to determine what tools you have on hand; and if you're lucky, you have a mentor who can give you a "heads up" about pitfalls and offer you strategies to use if you encounter them. Our audio book It's Your Move! *Transform Your Dreams From Wishful Thinking To Reality* is designed to act as both a source and a mentor.

Change is a lifelong process. That's why it's necessary to establish the groundwork for taking charge of your creative energy. The esoteric or hidden meanings of the Old Testament Creation Story and the twelve disciples in the New Testament reveal metaphorically how to use this powerful source of creative energy flowing in and through each of us.

The basic rules of the Creative Process—echoed in many sacred writings—are found in the 7 days of the Creation Story. The tools that assist you in your efforts to become a Conscious Creator are mental powers and are metaphysically revealed through the names and actions of the disciples of Jesus, a Master Teacher. Understanding the steps of the Creative Process and the nature of these spiritual tools available to you prepares the foundation you need for growth in consciousness.

Becoming a Conscious Creator

Becoming aware of the steps and the rules is just the beginning. Like we said, the process is not easy. It requires work to put what you know into practice. If you desire to become a Conscious Creator of your experiences, you will need to explore the nature of the work involved in your creative process. This work helps with the following:

- clarifying your creative efforts
- developing a proper receiving mechanism

Developing A Fearless Attitude

- learning how to make adjustments so that you can accept and receive greater potentials.

Doing the work is the discipline of becoming aware of the barriers that block your progress into better states of consciousness — barriers that keep you from recognizing that you are a creative being. This work is the discipline of shifting your focus so that you see the potential awaiting you, not the static you are currently creating.

It's Your Move! shares information that can help you avoid the boomerang effect your conditioning causes.

- Your life no longer has to be a closed loop filled with wishful thinking.
- That self-imposed circle can be broken.
- Your future can stretch boldly into the distance and be filled with new and exciting experiences as you become a mindful participant in the course of your life. Most people aren't, but you can be and should be! *It's your move!*

Developing A Fearless Attitude

BREAK OUT OF YOUR SHELL

After many years of working with a tribe in Africa, a retiring missionary gave the natives a sundial as a parting gift. Because of their great reverence for the man, the natives cherished the gift even though they didn't know exactly what it was. So they built a protective shelter over it, ironically making the sundial permanently useless.

Within each individual lie abilities, qualities, and potential that are currently dormant—essentially useless. The Apostle Paul said, "Stir up the gift of God that is within you." God gave us the gift of an unlimited life, and we have hidden it away, using very little of it. We need not fear depleting these gifts. It is only the limiting ideas of Man that create doubts and consequently create the atmosphere for all Man's problems.

Life is for living, not just surviving. Coping with life is not what you were meant to do. Limiting yourself, whether you do it by limiting your circle of friends, becoming set in your ways, or refusing to try something new, doesn't matter. What does matter is that you are sheltering yourself from life, enclosing yourself in a shell of your own making—a shell made up of beliefs that are rooted in weaknesses rather than strengths.

Think about the unborn chick enclosed in its shell. It is lying safely in its enclosure, oblivious to the outer world, but, like all of nature, it grows, expands, matures. Soon it discovers that the protective shell is actually limiting it. So it starts to peck its way out. First, it's just a very small hole, but it continues to peck until the hole is large enough for it to escape.

Are you content to stay inside your self-imposed shell, unable to grow and mature spiritually? Are you totally oblivious to the possibilities awaiting you? As long as you are unaware of your conditioning, your mechanicalness, you are living within a shell. As long as you are unwilling to step outside your comfort zone, you are living within a shell. You are living within a shell made up of your own limiting thoughts and feelings. Sooner or later, your inherent desire to reach for more will make you aware of the limitations of this shell.

Everyone tends to live within their ego. So it is not easy for us to admit that our beliefs, our personal wisdom are not enough. It is often when we find ourselves confronted with a crisis that real growth occurs. Like the chick who was forced to peck its way out of its shell in order to expand, we, too, find ourselves reaching for answers that lie outside our safe environment.

"Man's extremity is God's opportunity." This is just another way of saying that catastrophes, ill health, and tragedies are often the way you discover brand new beginnings. It is the pain that causes you to find the courage to seek something new, to stretch yourself, to do more than cope.

In the dictionary, *cope* is defined as "to strive or contend with successfully on equal terms, to be a match for, to match something, to stay on its level." My friend, you were not created to just make do, to equal the world around you. You were created to be an overcomer, an achiever, to expand your awareness of who you are as a creative being. Coping is identifying with your outer self and the world. Coping is reinforcing the limited version of yourself, the part of you that believes in the power of past conditions.

In Romans 2:1, Paul said, "Be ye transformed by the renewal of your mind." Psalm 8 says, "Thou makest him to have dominion." You are not expected to just cope with the protected environment from inside your shell. You were meant to have dominion over your life experience. That which is within you is greater than that which is in the world. The power and potential that is within you is greater than any problem or obstacle that the world can serve up for you.

Developing A Fearless Attitude

You can continue to maintain your shell of limitation, but eventually the divine spark within you will drive you toward a higher standard, making you aware of your shell's limitations. You will feel restricted, confined. These feelings will surface as pain because the shell is only made up of your thoughts and feelings. Often this pain drives people toward alcohol, drugs, and mental breakdowns because of their fear of breaking through their shell.

How do you break through your shell? You make a conscious decision to move toward a higher standard of life. Accept that you are constantly trying to expand, even if you're not aware of it. Take time to assess just where you have drawn limits for yourself. Pick out one of these areas and act upon it. Decide on a positive action.

Charles Fillmore said in his book *Prosperity*: "It is just as necessary that we should let go of old thoughts and conditions after they have served their purpose as it is that one should lay hold of new ideas and create new conditions to meet one's requirements. In fact, we cannot lay hold of the new ideas and make the new conditions until we have made room for them by eliminating the old. We are learning that thoughts are things and occupy space in the mind. We cannot have new or better ones in a place already crowded with old, weak, inefficient thoughts."

In other words, you cannot make room in your life for expansion if you are restricting yourself to a closed up environment. So get out of your shell. Learn to live life. Move through it with a spirit of adventure.

Developing A Fearless Attitude

TAKE A CHANCE ON OFF-ROAD EXPLORING

Have you had the experience of wondering if you had run a red light because you couldn't remember driving the last six blocks? Have you ever gone back home to see if you had locked the door or turned off the thing-a-ma-jig? Chances are, you did not run a red light, and the door was locked and the switch was off.

Why do we often find that something in us seems to do what needs to be done without our full attention? The truth is that we have conditioned ourselves to perform certain useful and necessary tasks without our conscious awareness.

Who's Doing the Conditioning?

The idea of conditioning is good in some respects because you can defer mundane tasks to automatic pilot and save your energy and attention for more creative endeavors. However, there is a downside to conditioning. While you can condition yourself through repetition to perform certain tasks, others can use the same procedure to modify your behavior on their behalf. As we mentioned earlier, the entire advertising/marketing industry functions on the premise that you are easily conditioned. They appeal most often to your emotional needs to be lovable, attractive, acceptable, and to your need to feel powerful and safe. Advertising is designed to persuade you that their product satisfies your need to comply with social norms. They successfully do this without your being aware that *they*—in the beginning—*created those norms!*

So, whose fault is it? Can you blame all your conditioning on the advertising industry? Unfortunately, no. Habitual, unconscious behavior is a psychological phenomenon called *scripting*. Under the influence of scripting, you *can* drive a car without running red lights, lock the door, and turn off the switch without any focused attention.

"What's wrong with that?" you might ask. "Why is our vulnerability to conditioning so important?" Because the power of scripting also **affects your thoughts and feelings, not just your behavior!** You fool yourself into thinking you always make conscious choices about what you do, say, and feel. You also think you know why you made those choices.

How Asleep Are We?

The truth is that all of us are asleep most of the time, unaware of the genesis of any of our experiences. The idea that you are not fully awake while walking, talking, and doing is definitely a blow to your ego. Your *only* hope for living creatively is to realize that you are asleep and to take responsibility for waking up. You cannot pass off your responsibility for living a conscious life by saying, "That's just the way I am!"

Cows created those famous erratic-appearing cow paths by avoiding anything outside what they could easily overcome. That's just the way they function. We often hear this kind of behavior referred to as following the *path of least resistance.* Most would assume then that the path of least resistance is not the path you should follow if you expect to experience change in your life. This is not necessarily true.

In my book *Metaphysical Minute,* I point out that there is more than one path of least resistance, and which one you travel depends on whether you are awake or asleep—whether you are making conscious choices or your conditioning is in charge. The "least resistance" can be the result of being on a consciously chosen path *or* the result of being on a familiar path—that is, one created by your conditioning and which no longer offers that many surprises or challenges you to change.

Your inner world supports your conditioning by creating in your outer experiences what you are willing to accept. Look around. Your world of experiences is mirroring back to you the contents of your mind and heart. When you recognize this, you understand why you find yourself in the same kinds of relationships, the same job situations over and over. If you don't understand this perspective, you look back over your life and declare, "That's just the way I am!"

How Do You Change The Path?

Nearly everyone is familiar with the Socratic quotation "Man, know thyself." Intuitively, you know this is a call for careful introspection. If you want to make your life more meaningful, you must be willing to challenge yourself on a moment by moment basis in order to wake up. Perhaps this is your time for *off-road exploring*. The roads may be bumpy or even nonexistent. The natives may be hostile (but they're all within you!). Sustenance could be sporadic, and there are no guarantees exactly where you will end up. But, I will guarantee you one thing: *You will begin to feel alive*—maybe for the first time in your life!

Overcome The Conditioning In Your Life

Are you ready to examine the choices you've made in your life and the reactions you have to situations? Unless you can commit to objectively viewing your past and present, the conditioning in your life will always be in charge. It won't matter what you think you want. It won't matter what you do. The power of your conditioning will be working behind the scenes to keep things as they are.

That sounds pretty fatalistic, doesn't it? If we refuse to acknowledge our conditioning, it is fatal to any desires we may have that step outside what we always thought we could accomplish.

The only path we have for upgrading our experiences is to open our minds to the thoughts and feelings we have each day. Then we can begin to question ourselves as to why we believe the way we do or feel what we do. Often, we have never consciously examined our beliefs. We don't know the genesis of most of them. Sometimes we are even shocked to realize that we believed such a silly thing!

These thoughts and feelings are borrowed from role models and others who may have had an impact on us for a period of time. Some of these ideas may have served a purpose at one time, but no longer. Yet, we haven't taken the time to discard them. Some of these ideas were destructive from the beginning. We accepted them because our parents or teachers believed them, and we deferred to their wisdom when we were young. Over time we accepted them as our own without question.

Some of these borrowed ideas cluster together and influence a person's entire belief system about his life and the world around him. As he encounters life with these beliefs as his lens, his own experiences will add to their strength. When a certain perspective is so prevalent, it leads to extremes. For example, bigots are often chips off the old block. Everything they see in their lives is filtered through the beliefs and attitudes they absorbed that make them bigots. That's why it is difficult to communicate with someone like this. There is no world outside that perspective. Because their minds are closed, they are unaware of their conditioning. Consequently, they are unable to view the world from any perspective other than that of a bigot.

Sometimes in life, a person can be caught up in a certain situation, such as being a victim. They are so identified with this mindset that when circumstances change, they still see themselves as a victim and are unable to let go of the past. They ignore the changes and ironically, they often begin treating others in the same way they felt they were treated. They are blind to the inconsistencies in their life because they are unable to release the dynamics of their past life, their conditioning.

Your conditioning is the single biggest obstacle standing in the way of improving your life. So how do you do something about your conditioning?

- You start by acknowledging the possibility that all your thoughts are not necessarily your own.
- Then you make a conscious effort to assess your attitudes about situations that arise in your life. It doesn't have to be a big event. It can be as simple as your reaction to the person in line in front of you at the store.

Once you examine the initial attitude and discover that it is backed up by lots of *other* attitudes—attitudes that you realize didn't start with you, you will be on your way to changing the character of your experiences and the quality of your life! Your journey of personal growth is the most important endeavor you undertake, and it can only happen by paying attention as you put one foot in front of the other.

Developing A Fearless Attitude

ⓞ Let's Talk About Subpersonalities

IS THERE A WAR GOING ON INSIDE YOU?

To truly understand this concept of subpersonalities requires discussion of many elements. Let's start by talking about your sense of "I."

We are all very much attached to our sense of "I." We take it for granted that the same "I" who went to bed last night is the same "I" who got up this morning. It is important to our sense of identity. It is even said that death is not dreaded because of the pain or the fear of the unknown, but rather because of the fear of losing your identity, your sense of "I."

As Maurice Nicoll teaches, the greatest obstacle to our spiritual growth is NOT realizing that we are not a single "I," but rather that we are multiple "I"s. Most of us resist the idea that we are not a single "I" because it feels like a threat to our identity. However, we can't help but notice the changes in other people. We acknowledge that they seem to be different people at different times, but we fight the idea that it is true for us as well.

Of course, when we see someone change, they are not really a different person. They are simply expressing different parts of themselves. It is these "parts" that determine or choose the roles we play in different circumstances. These parts are psychological formations within us that are seeking to express themselves. The roles we play are the result of which "part" or subpersonality is successful in taking center stage.

Something to think about: Have you ever wondered why it is so hard for you to take the passion for change you experienced at a seminar and apply it in your day-to-day life? Could it be that the subpersonality who was in charge at the seminar is not the one in charge during your daily routine?

Why does it matter whether we are aware that we are multiple "I"s or a single "I"? It matters because these subpersonalities don't just form for the heck of it. Let me ask you something.

Do you feel like there's a war going on inside you sometimes? Do you suddenly lose your confidence in certain situations or around certain people? Do you struggle between your desires and the voice that tries to hold you back? Those things you do despite your best intentions and those things you don't do because of those voices that stop you in your tracks belong to your subpersonalities.

Subpersonalities were formed at different times during your life by you. They were created to deal with situations that threatened you or made life easier for you in some way.

Are These Really Just Roles We Play?

Although people sometimes refer to subpersonalities as roles you step into, they are actually psychological frameworks through which you interact with the world and which choose the roles you play. Some people have created fancy names for some of the more archetypal ones. However, regardless of why they were formed or what you call them, the point is that their existence has slipped out of your conscious awareness into your subconscious and most of them have outlived their usefulness.

By being in your subconscious, they are able to take over your life without your even realizing it. You slip in and out of these subpersonalities without a single hiccup. In other words, you are making decisions from the perspective of a subpersonality that doesn't represent the Real You. When this happens, you are "asleep." The Real You is not making conscious decisions.

Failure To Re-integrate

Although you innocently developed these subpersonalities to help you through various difficult situations in the past, you failed to re-integrate them when the crisis or situation was over. Now there

Developing A Fearless Attitude

are so many that they take turns controlling your reactions to life while the Real You sits on the sidelines and dozes! The problem is that once they outlive their usefulness, they have no real direction and begin to negatively affect your life.

So, pay attention to these different characters who take center stage in your life. Observe each one and analyze why it acts the way it does. Then begin the work of making peace within yourself regarding the attitude that triggers this subpersonality. As with most things, it can take time, but it is part of your work on the path to wholeness.

RECOGNIZING YOUR UNIQUENESS IS THE KEY

We are all characterized by divisions in our personalities and have many in common with each other. However, you have to recognize your own uniqueness if you ever hope to move closer to expressing from the Real You.

All the instincts and tendencies of mankind are found within each of us. It is the *degree* to which they are active, mixed with the choices you make and the subsequent experiences, that makes you unique.

So when you encounter self-help programs that divide all the subpersonalities into neat little categories, remember that you are unique. Take the information and see if you can recognize any of the characters presented. This gives you a place to start.

From this point, however, you have to do the work of untangling the threads of your beliefs and experiences to determine how this subpersonality and others you will discover are influencing your life. You will then be able to work toward reintegrating each subpersonality by resolving the issues that are causing it to negatively impact your life.

Harmonizing Your Subpersonalities

There are five stages in harmonizing your subpersonalities: **Recognition, Acceptance, Coordination, Integration**, and finally **Synthesis**. Working through these phases is essentially linear. However, there is always an overlapping of action between phases. This is always true of any process involving personal growth. It is the result of new information impacting your actions and causing you to re-assess past actions.

The problems that arise with subpersonalities are a result of conflict, isolation, and competitiveness. Weaker elements within you (those you have not fed as often) give way to stronger ones more and more often, which will often lead to certain subpersonalities being in charge that are not appropriate for your best interests.

The goal is to create harmony between these psychological frameworks so that all their needs are met, which in turn will result in fewer negative emotions within yourself—emotions arising from frustration and disappointment.

Recognizing Your Subpersonalities

Recognition of your subpersonalities is vital if you are going to effect change; however, spending too much time trying to round them all up is counter-productive. Remember that the law of attraction is based on the energy that you invest in something. The more you invest, the greater the attracting power. In other words, if you spend all your time trying to recognize all your current subpersonalities rather than focusing on the changes you desire, you are actually feeding these subpersonalities and making them stronger.

Naming a subpersonality can be detrimental to your goals as well. If you name a subpersonality based on its negative attributes, then you may be contributing to the status quo. Think about this for a minute. When your family says things like: *You know you always get upset over little things* or *You've never been very good at making decisions*, don't you often find yourself getting upset or scrambling to make good decisions and consequently making bad ones?

Perhaps if you want to name your subpersonalities, you should consider the Native American approach to naming. Describe the subpersonality's potential. For example, instead of "The Lazy One," you might call it "The One Who Is Learning To Move Forward."

Trying to work on all your subpersonalities at one time will overwhelm you. Just pick out the ones that you instinctively know are standing in your way at the moment. Just like in setting goals, it is best to break it into bite-size pieces.

Developing A Fearless Attitude

Acceptance Of Your Subpersonalities

There are subpersonalities that we can term *healthy* because they tend toward harmonizing with your other subpersonalities. However, there are those who can be termed *troublemakers*. These subpersonalities are those that act out to serve their own needs without regard for the rest of your life's needs. They often act against each other.

For example, if you have a subpersonality that is seeking perfection in all that you do and another subpersonality that is constantly feeling that she is not good enough, then you can see how these two could play off each other. It is ironic because both may be working from the same erroneous belief about yourself: that you aren't good enough. The seeking of perfection in your work could be one way of reacting to this belief by striving to show the world that it isn't true. On the other hand, the second subpersonality accepts the idea that you are not good enough and focuses on pointing out all the ways in which you live up to this erroneous belief.

The troublemakers who are the most prominent in your life are the ones you need to embrace first. *Accept* that these negative attributes are the places where you can effect the greatest change. You do not want to reject the troublemakers or try to ignore them. This will only cause more conflict within you.

Remember that acceptance of your subpersonalities will be influenced by your own self-image. Those subpersonalities that support your beliefs about yourself will resist accepting those that are considered "less than desirable." However, as we discuss in our audio book *It's Your Move!*, it is important to dis-identify from these influential subpersonalities—to become objective.

All of these stages we're talking about will eventually lead you to synthesis, which is the highest order of organization within yourself—an order that helps you recognize higher impulses within yourself.

Coordinating Your Subpersonalities

The third stage of harmonizing your subpersonalities is coordination. Coordinating them requires that you recognize that each subpersonality has at its core a simple need that is good.

In order to coordinate these diverse subpersonalities, however, you will need to embrace each one to understand what its need is. Then you will need to use reason, communication, and compassion to discover a solution that will keep it from working against your highest good—a solution that will untangle the distorted ideas that are influencing its actions.

If you have a subpersonality, for example, that is contentious with others, you might begin by inquiring of this part of you why it feels that it must argue with everyone about everything. You will "hear" answers that will lead you to uncover why this part of yourself finds it necessary to take over your life when it does. This discovery will eventually lead you to the right solutions. These right solutions will make it possible for this part of you to stop feeling separate and competitive. It will begin to see that striving for that which is best for all parts of you is the best for it as well.

In other words, communication, reason, and compassion work as wonderfully in your inner world as they do in the outer one.

Integrating Your Subpersonalities

Coordinating your subpersonalities was about changing their "states of mind." The fourth stage of *integrating* involves the relationships between subpersonalities and ultimately how these relationships influence your *overall* state of mind and behavior.

Lack of harmony usually manifests in conflict, competition, and perhaps isolation. However, it is important to recognize that although you may feel that you are perfectly happy and well-adjusted, it may simply be that you have a dominant subpersonality that is repressing others within you. Because of this dominance, weaker subpersonalities are never able to express, and you assume that all is right with your world. The problem here is that you may be ignoring qualities or talents that could deepen your understanding and enhance your life experiences.

I mentioned before that *those subpersonalities that support your beliefs about yourself will resist accepting those that are considered "less than desirable" by them.* Thus, a dominant subpersonality may be able to ward off the expressions of any energies in your world that cater to other qualities. Eventually, however, these repressed subpersonalities will gain strength, and conflict will occur within you as they naturally seek to express.

This is often the case during times of depression or what some call the "dark night of the soul." It is a time when you may feel such a push-pull within you that you don't know which way to turn. The first step is to not panic. Knowing what is taking place gives you the power to choose how to handle the situation.

Recognize the players. Assess their needs. Analyze the benefits of each and how they can complement each other. Then make a conscious choice to cooperate with them both, allowing each to express when it is best for the real you. Often you will discover that their basic needs—the "good" at their cores—do not really conflict with each other. It is only the path of expression that is in conflict.

Synthesizing Your Subpersonalities

This is the point at which your growth as an individual begins. It involves the recognition, acceptance, coordination and integration of your subpersonalities in order to create a personality that expresses in a mutually beneficial manner. However, this is only part of the process of synthesis.

Synthesis is about carrying the same integration that is being achieved at the level of one's personality into your relationship with others in the world and into your relationship with your Higher Self.

Developing A Fearless Attitude

This process is about creating a new whole that is greater than the sum of its parts—one that leads to a new world, a new Universe.

⦿ Express Yourself

JUMPSTART YOUR SELF-ESTEEM

When we talk about increasing our self-esteem, we are often overwhelmed by the emotional and mental baggage we're carrying. So much so that we give up before we even get started.

All you need is an inroad to jumpstart the process, but tackling the way you feel or think about yourself is not easy. However, your mental and emotional natures are not the only ones you possess. You also have a physical nature, and it is much easier to access and change.

So let's begin here. You're probably thinking to yourself that I'm talking about becoming a work-out junkie, but I'm not. I'm talking simply about *body language.*

Body language doesn't just speak to others. It speaks to you. Allowing your shoulders to round over or slump forward—keeping your head tilted downward—avoiding eye contact ... all these postures tell your mental and emotional natures that you don't feel too good about yourself.

Don't believe me? For just a day, try walking with your shoulders back, your neck straight, your head level, and smile at others when they look your way. It will jumpstart change in your life.

Your body language will be transmitting to your mental and emotional natures that you have value, that you like yourself, and changes will begin to occur in those areas of your life as well.

Changing your body language gives you the opportunity to *experience* the feelings that accompany high self-esteem. It also changes the way others respond to you. This transforms your interactions, which in turn reshapes your emotional attitudes.

Keep this up and be alert to the changes occurring in your inner and outer worlds, and you will be on your way to healing your self-esteem.

Developing A Fearless Attitude

7 WAYS TO FIRE UP YOUR LIFE

Learning to express yourself means that you have to figure out how to fire up your passion, get a grip on what you want in life—all the things we are discussing to untwist your life. Take a few minutes to think about these 7 tips and how they can be applied to your life.

1. *Stoke Your Furnace!*

Wood must be added to a fire for it to continue to burn. If your life resembles a dying fire, find some positive idea, person, or interest on which to focus your attention.

2. *Exploit Your Weaknesses*

Weak muscles in your body respond to exercise and become stronger. Weak parts of your psychology are no different.

3. *Answer The Question*: What would I do if nothing stood in my way?

Once you answer yourself, you can begin the process of eliminating the limiting ideas you've placed in the road ahead of you. See possibilities, not barriers.

4. *Break Your Patterns*

Years of conditioning box you in. Use the scissors of your mind — your imagination — to cut through the bonds which hold you there.

5. *Pay Attention To Your Feelings*

Make sure you know whether your feelings originate inside or outside the box of your conditioning. Does your feeling seem terribly familiar? If so, ask yourself where responding to that feeling will take you.

6. *Step Out Into The Unknown*

Your imagination and your feelings guide your will or your ability to step out. So, proclaim your intent — muck up your courage — and turn your terror into triumph!

7. *Live For Yourself!*

Does a stream set out to nurture the environment through which it flows? No. It sets out to fulfill its purpose — to flow toward a larger body of water. The good it does is a by-product. You are the same. You can only influence those around you in a positive way by being true to yourself and moving toward greater spiritual evolvement.

Developing A Fearless Attitude

THE POWER OF PURPOSE

The power of purpose is akin to the concept of the rippling effect in the cosmos when a butterfly flaps its wings. It changes everything in the universe *because it changes you*, and you are an integral part of this magnificent creation you know as the Universe, participating in its unfolding.

Purpose Offers Creative Focus

Embracing a purpose gives you creative focus. It lifts you up to a new level of being and self-expression. It fulfills the truth that Jesus was teaching when he said, "And I, if I be lifted up from the earth, will draw all men unto me." Purpose can carry you beyond worldly aims. Following his *own* purpose, Jesus demonstrated that it is through your understanding of your connection to a higher source that you are spiritually uplifted, changed in vibration, or experience an increase in consciousness — however you choose to express it. Through this change, your interactions with the world around you are transformed.

Purpose Can Center Around Inner and Outer Work

Purpose often centers around outer works because these receive the highest accolades from others and boost your ego. However, these intentions are usually *not* the hardest to achieve. Because you can only demonstrate what you understand, the most essential purpose is one which takes place quietly and methodically within the inner world of your psyche. It tempers that which you desire to let go and embraces that which you desire to enhance.

This inner purpose establishes the level of your spiritual understanding as you patiently observe and adjust your interactions with your inner self and with those around you. Your outer works are measured and *enhanced* by the energy you expend in your inner realm. So, despite the intensity of your outer activities, *the only way to permanently alter your outer expressions is through your inner aim.*

Purpose may not always have a positive agenda even if it appears so on the surface. Using good works in the outer to validate yourself is simply an escape from the real work of investigating and reconciling the conflicting facets of your personality. The drive to do this inner work is necessary because you are the vessel through which Spirit flows into the world. Even the purest water is influenced by the vessel from which it is poured. A vessel filled with muck cannot dispense pure water.

This is why your works in the outer world will always correlate with the progress you are making in your inner world. You cannot *consistently* manifest or pour forth at a higher level of expression than the one which exists within you.

The Link to Your Creative Process

Purpose, whether focused inward or outward, is inextricably linked to your creative birthright. Developing a purpose requires your conscious use of the creative process that is metaphorically laid out in the seven days of creation. This creative process is the foundation for all your experiences, and it is always active, whether being operated consciously by you or not. The Law of Attraction is the impersonal force which brings your experiences into alignment with your focus in the creative process.

Having a purpose or intent in your life focuses your attention on the creation of a conscious desire. Thus, you are *actively* working toward the expression of your creative birthright. You are striving toward at-one-ment with Spirit. What greater purpose can there be?

What About Power?

Power? Yes, purpose has power. It makes you consciously aware of your choices and gives you opportunities to self-remember, that is, to rise above worldly aims and reconnect with the Divine. Eventually Purpose will demand that you embrace your creative

Developing A Fearless Attitude

birthright if its aim is to be met. However, the *true power* of purpose is that it ultimately brings you face to face with the power of Spirit.

Points to remember:

- Purpose can carry you beyond worldly aims to a new level of understanding.
- Outer works are *not* the hardest to achieve. They develop naturally out of your inner works.
- Don't think that good works in the outer are a substitute for your inner work.
- Purpose, whether focused inward or outward, is inextricably linked to your creative birthright.
- Purpose has the power to change your life.

Developing A Fearless Attitude

◐ Pay Attention To Your Feelings

ACCESSING THE MAGIC ENERGY

Have you ever noticed how difficult it is to grow your business when you spend most of your time in front of the computer screen typing or reading? Just as true is the difficulty of making new friends if you refuse to step out and participate in activities.

The reason is because there's a magic ingredient that's not accessible by you unless you are interacting face-to-face with others.

Make no mistake. It's real. Science tells us when two objects begin interaction, what was once *potential* energy (energy that was unavailable to us) becomes **kinetic energy** or energy in motion. Kinetic energy can be transferred from one moving or interacting object to another.

What does this mean to you? It means that when you go to a convention or a networking event, or you meet someone for coffee to discuss how you can help each other, or you meet with a Master Mind Partner, this simple interaction **unlocks energy to which you didn't have access before!** It suddenly becomes available for you to use. It increases your creative potential by giving you access to ideas from the collective unconscious.

You've felt this energy before. I know you have. It's that "high," that excitement you feel when you have personal encounters with people of like-mind. So, don't waste it!

Sometimes people let the kinetic energy dissipate without using it to their advantage because they don't understand what it is. Then they try to re-create it by going to more conventions or having lots of coffee dates. But, **it's only MAGIC if you use it when it's there for you!**

Don't mistake the activity that sparks the energy for its source, however. The source is spiritual and scientific. It is energy in motion.

This means you need to take action while it is in motion. Use it or lose it. Reach into the universe for the perfect idea that will take your business or your life to the next level.

Developing A Fearless Attitude

Useless, Unnecessary Suffering

Have you ever heard the expression "what you have to fight to get, you have to fight to keep"? It refers to *the use of personal will to force an experience into your life.* How can you possibly want something so much that when you finally get it, you have to fight to keep it? The answer to that question lies in your consciousness.

As I related in my book, *Metaphysical Minute,* consciousness "is the degree to which you allow all the power that is your birthright to flow through you into expression." One important element in the concept of consciousness is that it reflects the degree to which you are awake and aware of the Christ potential within you. There is another part of you that is not awake. It is known as your "false personality."

Your false personality is the part of you that is asleep to your divinity. It is the part of your psyche that is conditioned by the ways of the world. Unfortunately, your false personality is in charge most of the time—even sometimes when you think you are aware.

Your false personality is made up of all those *sub*personalities about which we spoke earlier that have formed over the years to meet your needs in dealing with the world around you. These subpersonalities manipulate your environment as well as your thoughts and feelings to maintain the status quo.

Therefore, it is possible for your false personality to focus its attention so intensely on a particular goal, doing anything and everything in the outer to *make it happen,* that you succeed in accomplishing the goal. However, this goal, achieved through manipulation by your false personality, leaves you expending tremendous amounts of energy trying to sustain it. If this happens to you, whatever the goal, it is not yours by right of consciousness.

Right of Consciousness

When something is yours by right of consciousness, it manifests in the mental realm first. It evolves from an understanding that creation comes from the within to the without. In other words, it flows *through* you into expression. Anything else is simply a manipulation of the material world and is temporary in nature.

How many stories have you heard about people who finally won the lottery only to be broke within a year? Have you ever known someone who literally clawed their way to the top? It's not unusual to find these people under a great deal of stress because they never actually developed the consciousness to sustain such a position naturally.

When you put material things or status ahead of your personal growth as a spiritual being, you have the cart before the horse. The only way to make reverse-thinking work is to pull the cart yourself, which takes an inordinate amount of energy. Energy isn't limited, of course, but the amount *to which you have access* is determined by your willingness to let your *consciousness* pull your cart, which is the natural way of things.

When something is yours by right of consciousness, it means that your internal creative process has drawn it to you, you are in vibrational harmony with it, and you have allowed the Universe to unfold it in your life. Maintaining it and expressing more of the same won't require huge energy reserves. The Law of Attraction will continue to draw experiences like it to you because it is now part of your consciousness.

Have you ever known someone who is always prosperous? Someone who, no matter what happens in the world, always seems to recover faster than everyone else without even trying? The place where they work closes, and within days someone offers them a better paying job. You know the people I'm talking about. Well, these things happen to them because prosperity is part of their consciousness. They don't fret. They expect these things to appear in their lives because their trust is in a higher power than the world around them.

So, don't commit yourself to a lifetime of useless, unnecessary suffering. Take the time to develop your inner world. You'll be amazed how much easier it is to deal with life!

Developing A Fearless Attitude

7 Sure-Fire Ways To Lose Everything

Do you have trouble achieving your goals? Do you feel like you have to stay on red alert just to maintain what you have? Are you unsure of your feelings about your goal? Then you need to take this quiz.

1. YES or NO - When your dream starts to spit and sputter like a choked up carburetor, do you give up? Do you assume it's a sign? Do you start thinking of reasons why no one else is willing to support your dream?

2. YES or NO - Have you decided that someone else will have to handle the part of the process involved in making your dream come true that requires you to do something you hate? Do you think that your dream will happen regardless of your fear?

3. YES or NO - Do you alter your dream based on what others tell you is "the way it's done?" Do you scale down your goal to escape the possibility of being disappointed? Do you make sure that your goals do not exceed your definition of reachable?

4. YES or NO - Do you feel that the methods you have used in the past when you tried to reach a goal are the best ones? Do you believe that the only problem in the past is that you failed to use the method correctly?

5. YES or NO - If your feelings tell you that something is wrong, do you assume it's fear and try to will yourself to carry on? Do you react to your feelings without questioning their source?

6. YES or NO - Do you always walk carefully toward your goal? That is, do you make sure that you know ALL the possible results before you try any new idea?

7. YES or NO - Do you believe that giving to others is more important than giving to yourself? Do you believe that nurturing

your own spirit is selfish? That "me first," no matter what the reasons, is wrong?

SCORE: If you answered YES to all of the above questions or even to 4 of them ... *CONGRATULATIONS!* You are definitely on your way to losing everything you are dreaming about! What manifests will not even come close to your original desire!

Addressing the questions presented in this chapter shows you how important it is to pay attention to your feelings and to break old patterns. You might want to go back and review the *7 Ways To Fire Up Your Life* in the last section (Express Yourself).

TIPS FOR HANDLING STRESS OR BURNOUT

Since stress is a common element in most of our lives, I have a few questions. *Are you cycling through feeling anxious, irritable or depressed? Do you have to push to stay in there? Are you tossing and turning at night? Has fatigue become your life partner? Are you easily distracted?*

Stress is defined as "a state of bodily or mental tension resulting from factors that tend to alter an existent equilibrium." I usually think of stress as a state of mind and view tension as a physical state. Since your mental world creates your physical world, let's talk about what goes on in your mind to create stress and ultimately body tension.

Causes of Stress

Your state of mind is swayed by many things.

- When you are stressed, you have usually allowed yourself to be **influenced by what you believe others expect of you.** This is often expressed through perfectionism, which is essentially trying to make sure no one can find anything wrong with what you do. This is an impossible task because if someone wants to find something wrong, believe me, they will!

- You can also be **in reaction to what has happened to date in your life or your business.** If things aren't going well, it's easy to justify ranting and raving about the state of your affairs. It's also easy to dismiss the accomplishments of others out of jealousy or frustration. All of these put you in a negative state of mind. This uses up a lot of energy, draining you and leaving little energy for positive movement in your life.

- You can also **sabotage yourself by making your environment unmanageable.** What does your desk look like? How many times a day do you get frustrated because you can't find what you're looking for? Is your appointment schedule too tight and consequently, you're always late?

- You can also **sabotage yourself by setting unrealistic deadlines**. When I say unrealistic, I mean deadlines that put too much pressure on you and are not necessary. Trust me when I say that the world is not holding their breath for you to get that page updated on your web site. The only ones judging you and reacting to something about your web site will not be that big a loss. There's a big target market out there, whether we're talking about business or friends, and you only want to work with those who are in harmony with you anyway. So don't let them be the source of stress for you!

Eliminating the influence these things have over you requires the discipline of self-observation that we talked about in the Spiritual Tools section. When you begin to feel pushed or stressed, ask yourself why. Are you pushing because of some unnecessary deadline or someone else's expectations? Are you making your life more difficult than it needs to be?

If you're honest with yourself and change your approach, you should begin to feel your stress lessening. Doing what feels good sounds naughty, but it is the path to mental recovery for those of us who have let stress take over our lives.

What Does Stress Have To Do With Burnout?

Stress usually occurs when you try to do too much for whatever reason or put too many expectations on yourself. It can manifest in a physical manner, such as unexplained aches and pains. It can also manifest emotionally, which results in hyper-sensitivity, emotional outbursts, anxiety attacks, etc.

If stress is viewed as an engine of activity, then burnout would be the point when the engine no longer has enough fuel to keep it going. Burnout is when you throw up your hands and disengage because you just can't get your mind around your life or your work anymore. Your emotions are so dulled that you're not even sure you are alive. You have no motivation, no hope. You have no idea where to turn or what to do. In extreme cases, life no longer holds much attraction.

Burnout is closely connected to certain types of personality traits.

- If you are an **over-achiever**, it may be difficult to ever succeed enough to recognize and appreciate the positive energy that comes from recognition or rewards for your work. It's never enough.

- If you have a **poor self-image**, your lack of self-worth can make you dependent on external reinforcement. Failure to receive it can lead to disappointment and, ultimately, burnout.

- An **under-achiever** can have various reactions to life and business. There is often self-doubt, anxiety, a fear of the future, a low tolerance for frustration, and possibly defiance if unable to achieve personal goals. Consequently, things such as the inconsistency of financial return with a start-up business can frustrate an under-achiever and lead to stress. If life circumstances demand that he/she must continue in place, ultimately, the combination of self-doubt, anxiety and fear of the future can result in disengagement or burnout.

Solutions

1. Implement some type of physical exercise in your life. Walking 3-5 times a week is the easiest way to begin.
2. Use strategies in your every day life that will nourish you.
   a. Eat 3 meals a day. Burnout or stress can cause you to overlook meal times.
   b. Get at least 7 hours of sleep at night. Use sound machines to help you go to sleep if necessary.

    c. Start accepting invitations from friends. If you don't have friends nearby, go to a coffee shop or the mall so that you are around people. Strike up conversations.
    d. If there is something you used to enjoy doing for yourself, like getting a massage or going to the park or watching a local ball game, then do it. Reading is a great escape from stress.
    e. Take 15 minute breaks during the day to regain your equilibrium.

3. Practice keeping a positive attitude about life. It's not easy to go from depressed to joyful. So initially, just try to live in a neutral place — a place where you're not negative. You may not be able to think of a positive stance, but you know you'll be open to it when it comes. Once you have cut yourself off from negativity for a while, the trip to joyful won't be so difficult.

4. Take time to analyze your life and your business. See if you can shed all the "I shoulds" and uncover more of the "I wants."

5. Determine if stress has created habits that are damaging to you, either physically or mentally, and work to stop them. Do you eat way too many sweets as a comfort food? Do you chew on your nails? Do you work 10 or more hours per day?

6. Explore your feelings about your connection to a Higher Source. Developing a conscious connection to Spirit can make a huge difference in your perspective on life. This is a highly personal experience. Don't worry about others' belief systems.

7. Develop a game plan based on the discoveries you've made about yourself and your true desires so that you can reclaim excitement, meaning, and direction for your life.

    So, set a goal this month to make yourself aware of how stress is impacting your life. Then tweak your life to get yourself back onto a creative and joyful path.

Developing A Fearless Attitude

THE REAL POWER BEHIND YOUR THOUGHTS

We talked earlier in the Spiritual Tools section about how and why we attract bad things into our lives. Let's ask ourselves another question somewhat related to this idea of your attracting power. Why do good people often have such a hard time and bad people seem to float unscathed though life? The answer? Life responds to what you think and feel you are worthy to receive regardless of how good or bad you are.

Many people don't realize that what they feel has more power to influence their life than what they think. In other words you can think about what you want, but until you feel you are worthy of it, you are "dead in the water." In other words, success has to happen in both your thoughts and feelings before it will happen in your experience.

The problem is that many people negate what they feel while at the same time trying very hard to transform their lives. This wouldn't matter except that a person's heart, the seat of their feelings, is the ingate through which what they desire must pass.

What does this mean? It means thinking about being successful is good, but until you FEEL successful, the most powerful ingredient to your success is missing. For example, most people want more money. However, if the books they read, the seminars they attend, and their personal examination do not break down this subtle feeling of unworthiness, they are not reaching the source of their problem.

Why do you suppose so many people attend workshops and seminars about how to make it big and yet few of them ever do? What I am saying is that you can think about being successful until "hell freezes over," but nothing will change. Attending a workshop that gives you the keys to being successful is great, but unless you reach an emotional agreement with what you hear, you will still be paddling a sinking boat.

Developing A Fearless Attitude

Does this sound too simple? Something you've heard many times before? Well, it's true! Success is an emotional reality before it becomes a physical experience! All the education in the world by itself cannot make you successful. Why? Because information alone can do nothing. Thinking about success and following the procedures that are supposed to make you wealthy means little unless it infects you with a feeling for the reality of being successful.

Am I saying that there is anything wrong with attending workshops on the techniques of finding success? No! I am not, but what I want you to do is be aware that your progress toward success is not totally dependent on using a technique. The techniques have the intent of giving you the feeling of success. However, your true feeling about being successful contains the real power. All the processes and techniques in the world are a waste of time unless they are backed by your feeling that they are building an emotional energy you recognize as the state of "being successful."

The bottom line is that your feelings are the real power behind your thoughts. Without them, your thoughts simply come and go. Your feelings energize them and generate motion in your life, and you'll see why in the next chapter.

Developing A Fearless Attitude

YOUR FEELINGS WILL BEAT YOU TO THE PUNCH EVERY TIME

Have you ever wondered why despite the fact that you said you were *not* going to eat that, say that, or behave like that anymore, you find yourself doing it anyway? The reason this happens is that ***feelings are 30,000 times faster than thoughts.***

Because your will power is driven by your feelings, you will often do the opposite of what you say you're committed to before you are consciously aware of it. In other words, you tend to do what you *feel*, not what you *think*. Of course, you can make a decision intellectually that is in total disagreement with your feelings. It doesn't mean, however, that you are going to be able to carry it out.

If you are going to deal effectively with the tendency that your feelings have to dominate your actions, you have to plan ahead to level your playing field.

1. Think about situations where you might end up giving in to temptation.
2. Come up with ways to handle these situations that will support the commitment you've made.
3. Take time to create a virtual reality. That is, imagine yourself in that situation reacting in this new way. Do this often.

The result of this exercise is that you are creating *harmony* between your thoughts and your feelings. You're developing the feelings that will help you sustain your commitment. So now when you encounter these situations, the feelings that will rush to the top will be ones that are in line with your thoughts (your commitment).

Let's say you are on a diet (and who isn't!). You are standing in front of your refrigerator, and behind the door is a chocolate cake. If you've already faced the fact that this is a place where your resolve will be tested, you will probably be all right. However, if you haven't used an exercise like the ones above, you may find your intellect telling you all about the value of maintaining your diet even as you wipe the last crumb off your mouth!

Developing A Fearless Attitude

PUT YOUR ENERGY WHERE IT COUNTS!

Have you ever found yourself wishing you could find a group to join or a close friend so you could experience that feeling you remember from some distant past, a feeling of really being in the flow of life? This is a normal desire.

As we mentioned in the chapter on Accessing The Magic Energy, when two or more persons get together with common interests or goals, often you can "feel" the energy. People have even been heard to say they get a "high," psychologically speaking, from being with certain groups of people.

AS we noted, science tells us that as two objects begin interaction, what was once potential energy (energy that was unavailable to us) becomes kinetic energy or energy in motion. So, it is the interaction of the objects which unlocks their potential energy.

In your personal world, the most dramatic results occur when this released energy is channeled toward a specific idea or goal. It can generate enthusiasm and creativity, opening doors you may never have considered before.

The Kinetic Energy Within

Within your psychology, there is a parallel action taking place when you strive to integrate the diverse facets of your personality into a self-actualized person. When you resolve inner conflicts, at least two of these facets of your personality are coordinating their needs toward a common goal. In other words, they come together. The textbook term for this is "overcoming a psychological barrier." You experience a sense of elation, joy, accomplishment, being in the flow of life. *This is released energy!*

If properly directed, this energy can be used to stimulate the process of personal growth. If you fail to recognize its potential, it fades away just as the light from a flashlight fades as the battery weakens. Your awareness of the energy that is available to you and the direction in which you focus that energy makes the difference in your life. It will not help you or those around you if you give all your energy away and save none for your own growth because you, too, will begin to fade.

Have you ever gone to a workshop on success or prosperity? The next few days you were so pumped up, utterly brimming over with the possibilities awaiting you. Two weeks later, you were just as depressed or unfocused as you were before the workshop, and nothing was changing for you. What went wrong?

You were catapulted into an emotional high from the initial energy released during the experience. **However, you wasted the energy trying to recreate the feelings of that *outer* experience rather than using the energy to open the door of *inner* communication for a greater understanding.**

Many workshops are presented on a "step 1, step 2, step 3" basis. There is nothing wrong with steps which create an outer discipline, but the information must be taken further. All levels of expression must be included for you to benefit from new knowledge. You must take the intellectual and physical aspects of this information and embrace them with your feeling nature so that a true understanding takes place.

This can only be accomplished by the individual. No one else can direct your energies toward personal growth except you. Without this final step, you may experience what could be called an "energy drain." It is accompanied by confusion, disillusionment, a general sense of discontent, and perhaps even a feeling of inadequacy on your part. This is because there is imbalance. You are experiencing the information through one of your mind centers— either the intellectual, emotional, or instinctive/moving center— which is currently in a negative state. For example, if your emotional mind, that is, what you feel, is the culprit, you must strive to function from your intellectual center, what you think sans emotions, in order to restore balance.

Taking Charge of the Energies

So, how do you take charge of these energies available to you?

You begin by understanding that you have an inherent drive to perfect yourself. Science calls this drive "**syntropy.**" It supports the idea of your being a self-improving organism.

The second concept you must understand is the very one which can undermine your natural tendency toward self-improvement. The diverse facets of your personality are often overwhelming as they work against each other within you. The nature of these *sub*personalities, as we discussed earlier, is separateness. Each has a different agenda it is trying to impose on your life.

For example: Let us say that you desire to focus your energies toward a more peaceful and prosperous life experience.

If you have a subpersonality that is an expression of anger, its agenda would not be interested in focusing on a peaceful lifestyle. Instead it would grasp every opportunity to express an angry reaction.

Another subpersonality that embraces the idea you're not worthy of success would not be willing to focus on your prosperity in a positive way. It would strive to focus your thoughts toward past failures rather than future possibilities.

Can you see the damage these subpersonalities can do if you allow them to be in control? If you invest minimal energy toward "perfecting yourself." then entropy begins to influence your life.

Entropy is the prevailing factor in inanimate objects, such as machinery. It is the tendency which causes forms to disintegrate or deteriorate to lower levels of organization, that is, to fall apart. We all know that machinery will eventually cease serving its function even if it is not being actively used. Lack of use or continued use, coupled with the principle of entropy, ultimately causes it to be unusable.

A machine never becomes more efficient or develops the ability to accomplish greater tasks than those for which it was designed unless man physically alters it in some way.

You, too, must deal with the effects of entropy. If you fail to use your talents, you soon lose the proficiency you once had. In the same way, if you fail to invest energy in your personal growth and understanding, you will cease serving a useful function with your life. Unlike a machine, however, you have the personal capacity for developing the ability to accomplish greater tasks and to become more efficient. It requires only that you invest your energies wisely.

Keep in mind:

- the principle of syntropy works for you
- the many subpersonalities within you have different agendas
- if you waste your energies, you are subject to the negative pull of the principle of entropy.

So it is imperative that you invest your energies into personal growth. To some it seems selfish to focus on your personal growth. This is not true. Focusing on your personal growth does not mean that you exclude all people and things from your life. It means that you are working on yourself so that you can be a better friend, a better parent, a better neighbor, a better employee. All of these things are by-products of personal growth. If you always focus your energies on the needs of others, you will eventually fade away, unable to sustain the energy necessary to fill their needs.

STRATEGIES

Strategies are important no matter what venture you undertake. You will most assuredly encounter obstacles along the way. In order to overcome them, you have to recognize your weaknesses and your strengths so you can utilize them in a way that supports your goal. You have to understand the most efficient ways to set goals. You have to recognize where you are and determine what you are willing to do, and ultimately, you have to be willing to redefine your life.

○ Exploit Your Weaknesses

IF IT DOESN'T DESTROY YOU, IT WILL MAKE YOU STRONGER

As you move through life, you meet problems of all shapes and sizes. Some are hardly worth mentioning; while others are life threatening or earth-shattering. Yet, they all have one thing in common. Each problem is merely the wrapping that hides a gift which has been custom designed to your specifications.

If you choose to entertain yourself in your life with the wrapping paper, the bow, and the box, that's perfectly all right. You can cuss them and discuss them. You can admire all the subtleties of their design. If, however, you are distracted by the problem—that is, the wrappings—you will never be able to receive the gift that was prepared especially for you.

The Gift

No matter what the problem is, the gift it carries has a peculiar quality. It cannot be delivered directly into your consciousness or your awareness. You must actively choose to acknowledge it and to accept it as your own. Only you can remove the wrapping, and only you can remove the gift from the box.

When you have a problem, that problem does not only exist outside of you. It is a part of your mental world; it actually emerges from the pattern of your thoughts and feelings. This is difficult for some people to accept because on a conscious level, they hold fast to the idea that they would not choose to be in their present circumstances. However, it is not that you chose the specific situation that has manifested. You simply chose attitudes that resonated with the "problem" that has manifested.

All problems serve one purpose. They cause you to focus your attention and give you the choice of either looking to the world for answers or looking to your Creative Source for answers. Problems give you an opportunity to change your perspective on your life.

Changing Your Perspective

Changing your perspective is a good thing because the one you now have has led you to the problem currently manifesting in your experience, regardless of whether that problem is physical, psychological, or social. Don't make a quantum leap, however, and assume for example that everyone has cancer for the same reasons, or that everyone who experiences bankruptcy followed the same path to get there.

Cancer, for example, is an extreme experience in that it threatens one's physical existence. Such an intense problem is an indicator that there is much to be gained spiritually if one is willing to look past the wrappings—the pain, the anguish, the fear of death, and the regret for things not done. Experiencing cancer may simply allow one person to redirect her focus so she can stop and smell the roses, reconnect with who she really is, strip away the persona and realize that the riches she sought were inside her all along. Another may learn the power of forgiveness because the cancer serves as a powerful metaphor for how her anger has eaten away at her and destroyed the quality of her life.

Despite the place of honor many give to suffering, it doesn't matter how much you suffer if you never look past the misery and embrace the gift it holds for you. If, instead, your suffering is your focus, it becomes what we called "useless, unnecessary suffering" and serves no purpose in your spiritual development.

If you choose to wallow in your problem, allowing your fear to overwhelm you, the problem will devastate you physically or psychologically. If you choose only to look to the external world for answers, you may force yourself into surviving the present experience, but the problem will return in some other form. Why?

Developing A Fearless Attitude

Because Spirit never gives up on you. God always offers new opportunities for you to embrace your wholeness.

To reach inside your box of suffering to take hold of a new idea, faith is required. It demands a belief in "the substance of things hoped for, the evidence of things not seen." It requires seeing something beyond the problem itself. The measure of your faith is your ability to acknowledge and accept that new idea into your world.

If you do choose to open the door of your soul inward toward God to search for answers, you will come out on the other side of this experience with a greater understanding of yourself than ever before, which is the purpose of your life on this earth.

You are here to learn how to express as a creative being, one made in the image and likeness of God, by continually availing yourself of every opportunity that diminishes the darkness cast by the belief in separation between you and God and you and others.

So, any problem that doesn't kill you, either physically or psychologically, does indeed make you stronger!

READY-AIM-FIRE

What follows is a technique I encourage clients to use when confronted with resistance or confusing choices. It is also useful when interacting with those who know how to punch your buttons.

It is always good to give yourself a chance to think things through before you allow your emotions to make all your decisions. As we know, emotions are 30,000 times faster than thoughts. So let's give our thoughts a chance when it comes to our decision-making. What do you say?

My Ready-Aim-Fire recommendation:

1. **Ready**: Allow yourself to stop FEELING for a few moments to break the force of the existing pattern or resistance. It's sort of like what Cesar Millan, the Dog Whisperer, does to break the state of mind in a dog. It interrupts the status quo. Since your emotions are faster than your thoughts, it is necessary to break that momentum.

2. **Aim**: Calmly and objectively assess all your options. Ask yourself which ones will take you closer to your goal or further from it. In other words, intellectually assess the options. Once you've made your choice (and remember, the choice is always yours, no matter what it is), then you allow positive, supportive emotions to align themselves with your decision.

3. **Fire**: Now you are ready to act, to be a conscious creator of your own life.

BELIEVE IN YOUR GOOD

There are times in our lives when we suffer a loss, whether in relationships, business, or just life in general, a loss that marks a turning point in our prosperity. We find ourselves looking back and feeling dismay that we somehow got onto the wrong path and have never been able to step back into the flow of life with as much abundance as before.

It is our focus on loss rather than gain that has created these experiences. If we can muster the courage to recognize what we have learned during those times of seeming loss and bless them, we are starting on the path toward a more fulfilling life. It speaks in the scriptures about "I will restore to you the years which the swarming locust has eaten..." This is our assurance that those years when we felt abandoned or despaired of ever finding our way back have not destroyed our good. Our good awaits our understanding. Our good awaits our acceptance that the wisdom we gained in awareness during those times is an important part of who we are today.

We must believe that our good was not destroyed or lost. It has only been our attitude, our belief in loss, that has blocked it from manifesting in our life. The only thing remaining is for us to declare fully our belief in divine restoration. Our good will be restored in God's time and in God's way.

⬤ Set Goals And Give Intention

GETTING OFF ON THE RIGHT FOOT WITH YOUR GOALS

First, before you do anything about writing a life goal, ask yourself if this goal satisfies a yearning in you. The things you often classify as yearnings are *directly* connected to your deepest desires.

These are also the things you tend to let slide. You busy yourself with so-called goals that are really **tasks** because you're afraid to challenge yourself with real goals.

A real goal is something that expresses your essence. In order to reach it, you will have to dig deep inside yourself — beyond all the garbage thinking you've been carrying around. You will have to believe in YOU.

So, is your goal tied to a state of being that describes at least one of the purposes you have in this life? For example, do you want *to be helpful to others*? Do you find when you are involved in something that expresses this yearning, you are deeply satisfied?

Then there's a good chance that it is one of the purposes you have chosen for yourself this lifetime. Some examples might be: to be financially successful (expresses a harmony with the energy of money), to be a successful entrepreneur, and so on.

**If Your Goal Is Tied To A Soul Yearning,
It Has A Power Feeding It Unlike That Of Any Other Goal**

So, how do you get off on the right foot with your goals?

- When you write a goal, do you take the time to make sure that it is not vague? Are you specific about what you want? Do you say "I want to own my own business and work out of my home?" Or do you state specifically what that business will be,

Developing A Fearless Attitude

describing it in such a way that there is no doubt what your desire is?

"I want to develop a retail business selling Arbonne™ cosmetics using my home as my office."

- Do you take the time to determine how you will know if you are being successful in relation to your goal? Define what success is to you. Is it so many dollars per month? So many clients? Whatever it is, you should clarify it for yourself.

"I want to develop a retail business selling Arbonne™ cosmetics using my home as my office. I intend to produce <u>gross sales of $5,000 per month</u>, and <u>have a customer base of 150 clients</u>. I also intend to <u>make at least one group presentation per month</u>."

Now that you've gotten this far, ask yourself the all-important question: Does this feel like an attainable goal for me? If it feels overwhelming, then lower the expectations that will indicate success to you.

DO NOT dump your goal. Simply design it in bite-size pieces so that you can accept it as being possible for you.

"I want to develop a retail business selling Arbonne™ cosmetics using my home as my office. I intend to produce <u>gross sales of $2,000 per month</u>, and <u>have a customer base of 75 clients</u>. I also intend to <u>make at least one group presentation per month</u>."

- Finally, be sure to establish a time frame. Remember what I said about being vague? Failing to state a deadline gives you an excuse to put things off.

"I want to develop a retail business selling Arbonne™ cosmetics using my home as my office. I intend to be producing gross sales of $2,000 per month <u>by September, 2015</u>, and have a customer base of 75 clients. I also intend to make at least one group presentation per month."

Developing A Fearless Attitude

Remember: When you are developing your goal, you are not alone. Your subpersonalities which make up what some call Monkey Mind are right there with you. They want to maintain the **status quo**, and the easiest way for them to do this is to *keep you from being specific about your goal.*

How does this work? Well, if your goal is vague, you experience a state of confusion about how to proceed. You can't really get your mind around the goal. This is when your *sub*personalities start to chip away at you until they crack your resolve. You have to be strong by taking charge and being specific about what you desire so that you can create a plan for reaching your goal. Every step forward you take with clarity moves you further away from the status quo.

Why Motivates Better Than *How-To*

Have you learned how-to yet? There are thousands of opportunities out there for you to learn how to do just about anything you can imagine. So why aren't you doing the thing you really want to do? I mean, if it's as simple as 7 steps to the life of your dreams or 3 sure-fire ways to get rich quick, WHY haven't you done it yet? Or if you have, WHY aren't you happy?

The *why* is actually the reason. If you haven't done it yet, it's probably because you don't know the *why* of it. **Why** is much more likely to motivate you to do something than *how-to* do it. If you go back to college, change your eating habits, or learn a new skill, it is the result of *why* you want the change. The *how-to* enters the process from the energy you invest in analyzing the *why*.

Even if you know the exact steps that tell you *how-to* do something, are you more inclined to do them without the added incentive of *why* you need to do them? I don't think so!

You can see that *why* you need or want to do something happens before you're committed to the how-to. In other words, **the reason your goal has value for you — the *why* — comes first.** Then you become interested in the steps involved in how-to achieve your goal second.

So, why do you sometimes achieve a goal without feeling like you've accomplished anything? Easy! You forced yourself to follow the *how-to* because you were pressured by expectations of yourself — from you and from others. This is common. It's human nature to want to do what is expected in order to be accepted. That's the reason you'll take a good-paying job rather than take a chance on the thing you really want to do.

Sometimes we're afraid that examining the *why* will take us out of our comfort zones. It might mean risking, and I don't mean financially. I'm talking about risking your perception of yourself and the perception you think others have of you.

For many people, the decision of *why* they do something is founded in seeking pleasure and avoiding pain. It is only when you decide on the reason why you should do something *regardless* of whether it brings you pleasure or pain that you are able to truly change your life.

The Connection to Your Creative Power

There is another important distinction between the *how-to* and the *why* of things. Determining how to proceed toward a goal is primarily an act of your **intellect**. Figuring out why you want to proceed is an act of your **emotional nature**. Your creative power is accessed through your emotional nature. So figuring out *why* connects you with your creative power! Then it takes the "how-to" and tweaks it until it fits you like a glove!

Following Others' Paths

People are sincere when they share with you the path they followed to success, but remember — that was their path, shaped by their creative power. It was their efforts in figuring out *why* that helped them *discover the power that was within them!* So, their *how-to* may or may not give you the ideas you need to express yourself — at least not until you unleash your own creative power by figuring out the *why*.

Beneath the surface of every one of us is a call to become something greater, stronger, and more creative. As that call is filtered through your everyday mind, it is usually misdirected toward the outer world. So the driving force in your life becomes the intellect — the *how-to* — rather than the *why*. Consequently, your creative power never has the opportunity to help you carve out your own unique path. Instead, you wind up trying to mimic the actions of others.

How An Idea Can Change Your Life

Each of us is a creative being. You are creating every moment of your life, and you use the same process to do so whether you are aware of it or not. It is through the act of commitment or intent that you *consciously* employ your creative power to take an idea and direct change in your life. Briefly, the elements involved are as follows:

1. You set **goals**, even if you set *no* goal. Goal-setting establishes polarity, an imbalance which the Universe will strive to balance through you. Your goals are your **ideas**.

2. Your **beliefs** determine to what you are able to say "yes," to accept as possible for yourself. Your belief system is the result of what has worked for you in the past, what you have accepted as true because it worked for someone else, or what you have accepted as the truth because it simply feels like it is true.

3. Your **enthusiasm** fires up your emotional natures [expressing positive energy or love for this idea] and your **imagination** is giving the idea shape and texture.

4. Your **commitment**, your intent to bring these ideas into wholeness, gives direction and momentum.

5. Your **knowledge**, the result of your experiences, assists you in discerning which things you believe will keep you on track to your goal.

6. Your imagination develops a **mental equivalent** of your idea or goal, the image which has taken form in your mind as a result of your use of the first five steps.

7. Finally, the idea becomes a **reality** as the Universe unfolds your creation.

The only problem is that we usually underestimate our power to create. We either do not believe we have this ability or we do not believe we can have what we desire. Neither of these attitudes is valid. You get what you desire every day by default. The process cannot be blamed if you do not set proper goals for what you claim you desire and commit to them.

If you are interested in more details about the creative process outlined briefly above, listen to our audio book *It's Your Move!* [http://www.WilliamsenPublications.com].

Developing A Fearless Attitude

ATTRACTING AND HARMONIZING WITH YOUR DESIRES

On television one Saturday morning I saw a cartoon character who swallowed a magnet. Suddenly appliances and objects zipped toward him. This comical episode, while just for fun and entertainment, is symbolic of a greater magnetic force that permeates every moment of your lives.

Universally applied, this greater magnetic force is a **Principle**, constant and unchanging. This principle attracts and organizes the celestial bodies into a harmonious synchrony. On a personal level, this principle is responsible for the kinds of people, amounts of money, life experiences, and the degree of health and well-being that you attract and with which you harmonize. You may be shocked to hear that the name of this force is **Love**.

The idea that Love is the force that attracts your experiences may seem strange, and it may offend the idea concerning Eros as a feeling shared between people. However, if you remember that *Love is an attracting, harmonizing principle*, you can see how it would tend to attract and harmonize you with others.

Well, if this is true, why do we tend to be so exclusive in what and whom we love? I'm sure you'll agree that you are inclined to be attracted to some people and situations and repelled by others. Unlike the magnet that attracts very specific kinds of metals, Love can create an affinity for anything or anyone, and this magnetic power will see to it that you experience your heart's desires. With your mental atmosphere—the thoughts and feelings that inhabit your mind, you draw forth your experiences from unlimited possibilities.

You're Calling the Shots

A principle is **impersonal**. For instance, the principles of mathematics and physics are the same regardless of who uses them. Do you think that math cares if you add 2 and 2 and get 5? No! If you should decide to stand on your head and gargle peanut butter, would the laws of physics care? No! Gravity would be your teacher.

Does the Law of Love care what you attract? Nope! You can create an affinity for anything. Remember King Midas? He created an affinity for gold. Everything he touched turned to gold, even that which he needed in order to stay alive.

Are you ready to take full responsibility for the consequences of your use of Love? After all, you created the mental atmosphere that has attracted your experiences.

Once you realize that the real obstacles lie within yourself, you have the necessary perspective for real prosperity and change. You stop trying to beat your world into shape and begin to look within to the real source of your good as well as your troubles.

- If you lack money, obviously you have not created the necessary atmosphere to attract it.
- If you continue to make contact with people who do not add to your social good, there must be something within that is attracting them.
- If your health is lacking, you contain within yourself the limiting idea of sickness.

The attracting, harmonizing power of Love is responsible for the movements throughout the galaxies as well as within your body. Scientists are discovering that it is the space between the smallest units of your makeup that hold the secrets they seek. These spaces are filled with the magnetic force called Love.

Developing A Fearless Attitude

STOP GROANING! IT'S GOOD FOR YOU!

Just uttering the word "commitment" to a group of people will elicit groans from all corners of the room. It not only smacks of hard work, but for most of us, it recalls all those times we've had to commit to things we didn't want to do. We were bound to our performance of some obligation, or we believed we were in the wrong place at the wrong time, or we were cornered into it. Putting aside all the groaning, **commitment** is a key to climbing out of the mediocrity or passivity of our lives.

Commitment literally means "a bringing together." That's exactly what it does. It brings together all the elements necessary for our success. If we have an idea that excites us, and we commit to it or give *intent* to do it, we unleash all the possibilities contained in that idea. Commitment *brings together* these possibilities with our beliefs, our enthusiasm, our knowledge, and our imagination, giving them direction and momentum. Otherwise, we simply have an idea — an idea which can only be described as inert or passive. Alone, it does not have the ability to create anything in our lives.

The Creative Process

Each of us is a creative being. We are creating every moment of our lives, and we use the same process to do so whether we are aware of it or not. It is through the act of commitment or intent that we *consciously* employ our creative power to take an idea and direct change in our lives. The elements involved are described briefly in the earlier chapter titled "How An Idea Can Change Your Life."

To quote that chapter: the problem for most of us is that we underestimate our power to create. We either do not believe we have this ability or we do not believe we can have what we desire. Neither of these attitudes is valid. We get what we desire every day by default. The process cannot be blamed because we do not set proper goals for what we claim we desire and commit to them.

Depth of Commitment

The *depth* of our commitment determines the number of the avenues through which our goal can manifest and the level of manifestation. Measuring this depth is not a scientific process, but there are certain criteria. Depth is determined by the use we make of our **emotional, intellectual, and moving centers** in our efforts. If we are identified with one center or the other, it creates an imbalance, which jeopardizes the outcome of our goals.

- **Do you approach your goal "in your head?"** Do you gather information, desire to know all the "ins and outs" concerning the topic, and sort through all these things to create a foundation from which to work? Do you spend all your time analyzing the details and fail to take the first step?

- **Do you approach your goal "with your heart?"** Do you look around at others and feel envious of their success, doubting your ability to achieve your goal? Do you find all sorts of reasons, which can fall under aesthetic, religious, or moral, as to why it will never work? In other words, *it's not good enough; I shouldn't be focusing so much on making money; I shouldn't be taking time from my family on what's probably a dead end.* Do you just want it so badly that you are going to go for it whether it makes sense or not? Are you unwilling to look at the risks?

- **Do you approach your goal like a "bull in a china shop?"** Do you just start in without thinking it through or determining how you really feel about it? Do you focus only on getting it finished? Are you constantly having to redo things because they don't work?

Functioning from all three centers — intellectual, emotional, and moving — in a balanced manner achieves a full depth of commitment. Most of us do not practice this routinely because we tend to mechanically operate from one center or the other. However, striving to be aware of our approach to our goals will enhance not only our goals, but also our daily lives. Knowledge (intellect) cannot stand alone. Truth, which is revealed through our emotional nature because we recognize Truth through the emotion of love, cannot stand alone in this creative process either. Conscious creation requires the capacity of the intellect, the power of the emotions, and the vehicle of our biology.

Quality of Commitment

The *quality* of our creation, however, depends upon the amount of wisdom we utilize. Wisdom is fully available to us through taking on the mantle of Spirit. Through this wisdom, we will:

- only strive to create situations in which there is no loser
- not win at the expense of someone else
- recognize the journey of each and every person as equally important as our own
- understand that our journey affects theirs and vice versa
- honor the rights of others to experience their life lessons instead of trying to mold their lives to fit in our own "box"
- understand that there is honor in the journey.

Conscious commitment is an important *key* to moving out of passivity — moving toward a more active, creative life experience. Commitment gives direction and movement to our goals by bringing together the elements of the creative process and giving us an opportunity to consciously use our intellectual, emotional, and moving centers to express our goals more fully. However, donning the mantle of Spirit and accepting the wisdom available to us helps to broaden our view. This process benefits us and others because it always results in a win-win situation. The decisions may not always seem so to us because we cannot be in the minds and hearts of another, but we must always seek this wisdom and seek to do no harm. This wisdom will not allow our intellect to rationalize or our emotions to "bleed," causing us to do things which interfere with the journey of another unless it is appropriate.

The imbalance, the polarity, we create by our original intent or commitment, if the intent is made through wisdom, will result in a tenfold return. This return will not be in a prescribed material form. It will be in the form of the love energy, which is the essence of all that we could ever hope for. It is the energy that *powers* our creative processes.

So, stop groaning. Commitment is good for you!

Use Wisdom To Achieve Balance

Many are familiar with the concept that "thoughts are things." It affirms that your reality forms first in your mental world. What this short statement does not make clear is that nothing is ever created by the energy of thought alone. There are three forces necessary for manifestation or the creation of your desire:

- One is your idea, your thoughts;
- Two is the emotional energy you invest in those thoughts; and
- Three is the harmonizing force.

Every creation requires all three forces. Your thoughts will simply float unless you invest emotional energy in them. The nature of the emotions you invest will determine the nature of your result. Any counter-productive or negative feelings or thoughts that are part of the mix can have a devastating effect on your creation if you are not aware of them. They can dilute your manifestation to the point that you don't even recognize it, or they can neutralize your desire so that nothing seems to happen.

That's why the third force is so important. This is when the intense work of change [personal growth] can take place. The third force synthesizes your idea based on the balance you achieve between your thoughts and feelings. So your awareness of the quality of the thoughts and feelings influencing your decisions is essential if you want your idea to be more than wishful thinking.

You have to use your inherent wisdom to discern which of your thoughts and feelings conflict with your conscious desire. You have to be aware enough to realize when you are coming under the influence of such negative thoughts or feelings so that you can consciously shift your attention toward what you desire. Don't waste your time trying to figure out why some negative belief exists in your mind because it's not necessary to fortify yourself against it.

Developing A Fearless Attitude

Invest your energies instead toward recognizing these types of thoughts and feelings and steering your attention back toward your desire.

So, as you embark on a new creation, remember that once your emotions are invested in an idea, you *will* create something, but it will reflect the *balance* reached between your thoughts and feelings. So, if you really want this new creation, honestly ask yourself:

- Are my thoughts and feelings counteracting each other?
- Am I even aware of what my true feelings are?
- Are there thoughts present in my mind that do not support my desire?

Becoming a Conscious Creator is the only way you can actively influence the end result. You must aggressively engage in sifting and sorting your thoughts and feelings and keep your eye on your goal. Otherwise you spend your time wondering why life is so unfair. *After all, you worked hard on your project.* Unfortunately, it doesn't really matter what you do in the outer unless the proper balance is struck between your thoughts and feelings, and this requires intense conscious effort. Thus, the really important work is done within.

Thoughts and feelings and the balance that exists between them have been the topic of philosophical / psychological discussions for centuries. Achieving a functional balance requires acknowledging that *psychologically* you are androgynous, both male and female. Denial of this truth creates conflict within your own psychology and in your relationships with others. This ageless concept is described in the *eros* and *logos* of the I-Ching, the *yin* and the *yang*, and the *anima* and *animus* of C.G. Jung as well as in the metaphorical stories that relate the formation of humankind in sacred writings.

The animus or the masculine energy is represented as the intellect or the thoughts. The anima or the feminine energy is represented as the emotions or feelings. Understanding how these

Developing A Fearless Attitude

energies impact your life requires releasing all biases and societal conditioning regarding the sexes so that you observe these energies in a purely psychological context.

All of the concepts mentioned are related to wholeness. If you view the word *androgynous* in terms of wholeness, you must recognize that anything which is androgynous **includes within the whole both elements necessary for creation**. Therefore, from a purely psychological perspective, you are androgynous. You are whole, containing within yourself the energies necessary for you to function as a creative being—in other words, the two forces I mentioned earlier.

Bottom Line

So, the bottom line is: You have everything you need to create your goals within you. You just have to make the effort to understand how the energies work together and learn how you can fine-tune them to achieve your desire. You are inherently a creative being, that is, always creating your life whether you are aware of it or not. So, why not invest the necessary effort to understand the process through which your life unfolds?

Developing A Fearless Attitude

◐ Step Out Into The Unknown

LOOKING OVER YOUR SHOULDER

Can you believe how far we've come into this new millennium? I can remember the hoopla around the turn of the millennium as if it were only yesterday!

Looking back can often bring up a series of regrets. This is not a good thing because it takes you back into an old energy, an old way of perceiving and thinking. Why does this matter? It matters because it can drag YOU backward. It can dredge up and activate negative attitudes that you have been working to release.

We are in a time of great change as humans. The key to permanent change is to recognize that you cannot hold onto the past. Release it in whatever form it takes. It may be represented through

- hoarding of things to keep the past safe
- attachment to memories of past efforts to reach goals that failed
- attachment to an image you have of yourself based on experiences and what you believe are others' ideas of you
- constant stirring up of old fears that emerged from the past.

Can you see how ALL these things have a vibration or a feeling attached to them that holds you in the past? How can you expect to move into a NEW way of thinking, feeling, and responding if you refuse to shed the OLD?

It's not possible for the same reason you can't put new wine into old wineskins. If you truly desire change in your life, then you are saying that you want to let go of the old understanding and the old relationship you had with life. You want to vibrate or interact with life at a higher level. You want to see greater possibilities and reach for your highest potential.

Developing A Fearless Attitude

You cannot do this except by looking forward. If you continue metaphorically looking over your shoulder by hanging onto the past out of fear of losing who you are, you won't have the strength to move forward because your baggage will be too heavy for you to carry.

Developing A Fearless Attitude

WHAT IS THE COLOR OF YOUR UNIVERSE?

In the process of your personal growth, you are constantly having to re-interpret experiences in your life. In other words, you have to take your experiences into your mental world and process them again to gain a more objective view — one that is free of the emotions in play at the time the experience occurred.

For a conscious creator, this is extremely important because you are always encountering new information and stepping into unknown arenas. It's only natural that some of these experiences appear to be confusing or ambiguous.

Remember seeing those figures that perhaps looked like a beautiful woman one moment and an ugly hag the next? Well, through using such figures, studies have shown that after a person was asked to view the image *only* in their memory, they were better able to view the alternate figure. The same is true for you.

The best results come when you take your experience into your mental world and consciously review and re-interpret them. When you do, you're able to gain a new perspective of your life or your business and your place in it.

Your experiences increase your knowledge, and your reviews of them will increase your understanding. The bottom line is that the color or the character of your Universe shifts as your vantage point of life changes.

The process of becoming an enduring, successful conscious creator requires the process of personal growth. If you deliberately engage in this process of review and re-interpretation of your experiences, you will never react quite the same way again to situations in your life. It influences your behavior in all areas of your life. The change may not come in large increments, but it will come.

You Can Never Go Back

Once you start this process, you can never go back. I don't just mean that you can't stop reviewing and re-interpreting your life. I mean that you can never go back to your *previous level of understanding*.

Have you ever gone back to a physical place – your home town, your old high school – and found it didn't resonate with you the same way you remembered? What about friends from another time? Getting back together with them is often uncomfortable because you find that you don't view each other or the world today the way you did before. You have to make adjustments and establish a new reference point with them.

The same is true of your experiences when you engage in this process we're talking about here. The next time you have an angry customer or you're in unfamiliar territory, you won't be able to respond in the same way you did before because your current understanding provides a different vantage point for you.

The Process

Let's take a moment to consider the process for doing this. Whatever belief that you now hold, that perception—that understanding—will be the filter through which you interpret any relevant experience or confusing concept. So, how do you shift your perspective so that you gain a new understanding — so that you are able to re-interpret the circumstances?

You have to be open and receptive to the flow of energy into you from your Creative Source. You have to be open to *everything* that crosses through your mind and enters your experience. Allow each piece of information to have importance.

It doesn't mean that you *act* upon everything that enters your mind or comes into your space. It simply means that you don't dismiss it as trivial or stupid. To intuit the knowledge that flows to

Developing A Fearless Attitude

you, you must be in a *receptive* state of mind. Often it is like playing the game of Clue. Seemingly innocuous thoughts will suddenly link with others until you experience a radical change in your perception.

This change in perception is the re-interpretation of that original belief you held. You now see in a new way. You see how your original belief connects to other pieces of knowledge that you never considered before. It opens a new doorway to you, and your world looks different.

So you see, you really can't go back to your old ways of thinking when you consciously engage in the process of growth.

Are You Willing To Step Into The Unknown?

Neither you or your business life is a stagnant organism. Each is changing. The direction of that change is up to you, however. Are you willing to step into the unknown? This is a *huge* question because growth implies change, and change implies something different, which suggests something previously unknown or not experienced by you. So your willingness to step into the unknown is critical for elevating the level of your success and also for establishing its staying power.

My suggestion to you today is to look around you. What is the color of your universe? Is it filled with the gray of uncertainty? Has the red brilliance of your passion faded into a reddish-brown hue of negativity? Perhaps you're beginning to see healing hints of green around the edges of your world. Maybe even golden flashes of wisdom sporadically color your reactions.

Whatever the character of your life, you have an opportunity to create a better experience for yourself by actively engaging in the work of shifting your perspective — shifting your perspective so that your life experiences are not filtered through those conditioned reactions that keep presenting you with the same experiences over and over.

Make "conscious choices" your filter for every event in your life. Do not judge these events by past experiences. Instead, forge ahead courageously with your newfound understanding as your mentor. You're the artist. Decide on the color you want your universe to be.

Developing A Fearless Attitude

RISKING: LIVING WITHOUT A NET

Risk (risk) n. *exposure to the possibility of injury or loss or to a dangerous occurrence.*

When most people think of risk, they don't consider it the *possibility* of an undesirable event occurring. They consider it a *probability!* Why do we make that subtle shift and give support to the idea that risking will always result in loss?

As children, you were warned against all sorts of dangers by your parents and others who meant well. How many times were you told "Don't cross the street by yourself for you'll get run over"? Not that you might possibly get run over *but* that you would in all likelihood be history! This leads to a pattern of avoiding anything which is unfamiliar or is not accompanied by an obvious escape route. Often, it leads to the implementation of tremendous amounts of structure in your life as you mature. You are resistant to change because **change is always accompanied by the risk of the unknown.**

This is unfortunate because too much structure leads to rigid thinking and a boring, uneventful life. To have diversity and serendipity in your life, creative juices must be flowing. However, too much creativity without some structure leads to chaos. So, there must be a balance of the two. This is necessary for any risky venture.

How would you define risk in terms of your business life? More important, let's determine what it isn't. **It *isn't* seizing upon an idea and jumping in feet first.** As I said, it requires structure and creativity. First comes the idea. For example, you decide that your department needs to be reorganized because the current organizational model isn't working. Your production is mediocre, and the staff members are not contributing any more than absolutely necessary. So, do you just go in on Monday with a new organizational chart, inform everyone of the changes, and walk away? If you try this, you would be putting risk into the *probability* category for sure.

Developing a Course of Action

If you want to risk making a change, you have to develop a course of action based upon the results you desire. If you only know that you don't like what you have and want something different, you are taking the biggest risk of all!

In the business example above, you have to set clear goals for your department. These goals can include organizational styles, production levels, interactions, as well as communication and motivational levels. It should include everything you consider important to the vision you have of your department. Once you have a clear vision, it is important to recognize at what level your department is functioning at the present. What do you think the problems are? Be specific. These two activities involve creating **structure**.

You might want to look at it in terms of remodeling a house. You have an existing house with walls and all sorts of in-place connections for plumbing, electrical, and so on. You don't want to move or tear down the house. You want to remodel. So you will have to deal with some of the elements that currently exist and decide how you can improve them.

Next, you use your creativity to actually develop a new plan. You develop a plan that incorporates all the elements necessary for your department to reach the goal.

- The plan should address the problems that currently exist.
- Your plan should establish new functional relationships, better using the skills of the personnel and developing a sense of cooperation rather than subordinacy.

Developing A Fearless Attitude

- The plan should streamline the overall process and increase production without increasing overtime.

You then present your plan to the staff for feedback. You are mindful of all their comments and suggestions. You adjust your plan where necessary. All these efforts involve **allowing for the creative flow**.

Risk Always Requires Courage

You have now balanced the elements of structure and creative function. You are focused on the end result you desire. You have gathered the forces of the others who must support this idea. You may want to ask, *Is the implementation of this plan a risk?* Of course, it's still a risk! Change of any kind is a risk. The process of balancing structure and creative function does not remove the risk factor. It simply ensures that the risk remains in the realm of possibility *rather* than being highly probable. That's the best handicap you're going to get.

Remember how exciting it was at the circus to watch the trapeze artist who flew without a net? Imagine the courage it took for him to slip his fingers off that bar with no net and his colleague's fingers just out of reach. Even though he had practiced for many hours with a net, when the lights went up, he had to be willing to **trust the structure** created by his practice and the creative function of **his own abilities** to lead him to success *without* a net.

To experience an invigorating life — personal or business — we have to have that same type of courage. The Old French origin of the word "courage" means mind, heart, and spirit, and it is from these places that structure and creativity emerge.

Developing A Fearless Attitude

◐ Redefine Your Life

EVEN BABY-BOOMERS CAN REDEFINE THEIR LIVES

This article is for you baby-boomers out there who are redefining your lives because what you were doing doesn't excite you anymore or isn't part of your scene anymore for whatever reason.

Baby-Boomers, now is the best time in your life!

Let's list some of your assets.

1. You've lost some of the illusions about what life is about, and you're willing to open yourself up to new ideas and experiences.
2. You have a wealth of life experiences to support your decision-making processes. This alone is a valuable asset.
3. Because you've worked in many fields or at least one for a long time, you have a clearer vision of what you do and don't want.
4. You don't have to think about raising a family and putting them through college anymore (at least most of you don't!).
5. You developed people skills at an early age because you either had to talk to people on the phone or in person. There was no such thing as emailing! So, you had to learn social graces.
6. This one may sound catty, but it's not meant that way. You learned to communicate in writing with the use of full sentences. Business correspondence was a formal business letter with proper punctuation and grammar.
Many people today have grown up communicating through IM or email shorthand. Unfortunately, it often transfers into their more formal communications. In most successful circles, a more professional approach is still required.

Pretty good list of assets for starters, isn't it?

Developing A Fearless Attitude

The biggest challenge to most baby-boomer entrepreneurs today seems to be technology. No, you're not having trouble learning it. You just think you have to understand it *all*. Before the onset of the internet and home computers and the explosion of related technology, most people believed that their challenge was to learn everything about the job they held. Mastery of domain-specific knowledge is not that difficult to achieve. You can learn nearly everything there is to know about carpet cleaning or transmission repair or dental ceramics. However, trying to keep up with all the computer technology that enters your world these days as an entrepreneur in addition to the domain-specific knowledge can feel overwhelming!

Starting a new job within the last year is considered a major stress trigger. When a friend of mine mentioned this the other day, I laughed to myself. Every time I start a new project, it feels like I've started a new job! It seems there is always some new software program I have to learn or some new marketing technology that is a *must* now. Although I have come to expect this, there are days when I would like to rest on my laurels, so to speak. I would like to feel that I have learned enough in the technology department to carry me for a little while — at least long enough to spend quality time working with the domain-specific knowledge that I have! After all, that's why I started down this particular path in the first place.

So how do you deal with it?

- First, count your blessings—all those assets I listed at the beginning.

- Give up the idea that you can keep up with all the technology out there because you can't, and you don't need to.

- Don't be afraid to ask for help. There are a lot of people out there who make a living doing some of those things you don't know how to do. Take advantage of it. If you don't have the funds to do that, ask around. There is usually someone out there who will barter with you. You're not the only one short on funds.

- Don't try to be a perfectionist! Learn as much as you need to accomplish the task that will support the success of your business, and then move on.

So, Baby-Boomers, I would say that the cards are stacked in your favor. You just have to take stock and make a plan and then stick to it.

There is one last thing that I hear Baby-Boomers talk about. Because you have had such diversity over the years, you have experienced failures as well as success. So, sometimes it is tempting to look at all the possible things that could go *wrong* with your dream and give up rather than focus on the possibility of success.

Remember to judge today's dreams by today, not yesterday!

Developing A Fearless Attitude

CAN DE-CLUTTERING REDEFINE YOU?

Something that always arises in the early months of the year is the desire to de-clutter. It can also arise when you reach a point of desperation with your surroundings. De-cluttering in itself is neither a good thing or a bad thing. It is the attitude you take toward the process that makes the difference.

If you're lucky, there's only a year's worth of stuff to ponder. For most of us, however, decades' worth of stuff that we have been hanging onto for one reason or another awaits us.

What's The Obvious Benefit Of De-Cluttering?

Well, you can open the closet door without an avalanche of junk falling on your head. Your office files will start to be more relevant to your business today, and you actually have room for new files. You can locate things more easily. You feel a sense of achievement when you look around.

But ... is that enough? It's a quick high, and it does feel good! However, de-cluttering can serve a much higher purpose if you take a different approach psychologically.

So What Is The Best Approach To De-Cluttering?

As you go through your stuff trying to decide what to keep and what to toss, whether it's personal or business, be aware of the feelings that arise. The most prominent feeling is usually fear. Let me give you an example.

My husband and I rented a 10x10 storage unit when we moved to Atlanta. During the next four years, I gave away enough of it to scale down to a 5x10. Then several months later, we moved all the boxes we had in storage to the house. It is important for you to know that I have been hauling some of this stuff around for years from one city to another. It's true that in some of those places I was able to use a lot of these things. However, we downsized, and it is unlikely that I will have a place to display them anytime in the near future.

The question for me became - *how important is it for me to keep these things? Is it important enough to dedicate a whole room to storing them?* That was sort of a "Duh!" question, but it was still difficult to address the idea of getting rid of the items that remained. So I began the journey of going through each box. I was committed to the idea that I couldn't keep hauling these things around. I have no children to whom I can pass them down. So I divided them into three categories: junk, good stuff that I don't really need, and stuff I still want.

The difficult part was that some of these things were woodcraft items my parents had made. Releasing most of these things brought out the fear that I was losing a part of myself, a part that I could never regain. I felt that I should hold on to them. Other things brought forth the fear that I might never find something else I liked as well.

I started thinking that maybe they didn't really take up that much room. After a couple of hours of not making much progress, I realized that this whole idea of de-cluttering was really about TRUST. Did I trust that God, the Universe, will supply me with what I need when I need it? Did I trust that I was more than the sum total of a bunch of things, no matter how sentimental I felt about them?

So at that moment I had a choice to make. The junk pile went into the garbage. The good stuff that I didn't really need and some of the stuff I thought I wanted to keep became my "give-away" pile. So I gave most of the sentimental things to a friend, who has three children so they could enjoy them as a family. Some went to my siblings. The others I gave to people who lived around me. When all was said and done, I had reduced my "stuff" by two-thirds!

Developing A Fearless Attitude

Was The Cardinal Benefit Of De-Cluttering Gaining Extra Room In My House Or Just Making It Easier To Find Things?

Neither. It was taking the step to let go of the past, the familiar, so that I could fully trust in the "evidence of things not seen." It was an outer expression that helped me better align myself with what I say I believe. It was a way of getting my thoughts, my feelings, and my actions into harmony with each other so that I can manifest a better life.

Hopefully, you can do the same. We cannot say that we believe in the abundance of the Universe and continue to hold onto the past, to things we don't need, in fear that we will be left with nothing. Such fear counteracts or neutralizes our belief and leaves us in a void that is not satisfying.

Start this year, this month, this week off right. Release those things in your life that have no value for the life you desire or that make it impossible for you to step outside your comfort zones.

Redefining yourself is an important strategy. Do not attach a judgmental attitude to this process. Instead, use ideas such as reevaluating your beliefs, rethinking your attitudes, reinventing yourself to better express your passion, reconsidering your current path, revisiting your reasons for your choices. However you choose to approach the process of redefining yourself, make sure that you see it as forward motion, as a means of developing a fearless attitude.

REVIEW QUESTIONS: DEVELOPING A FEARLESS ATTITUDE

1. What are the reasons that it is important for us to remain teachable no matter how old we are?
2. Why is it important not to sit back and let others determine your path in life?
3. Why is it important to take charge and stretch yourself when setting goals?
4. Do you let the "facts" that others offer you become the basis for your decision-making?
5. Do you understand the difference between a carnal person and a spiritual person?
6. What gives us the opportunity to make choices which impact the clear expression of God flowing through us?
7. What did you come into this plane of existence to do?
8. What is the most difficult part of changing your consciousness?
9. What often derails the manifestation of one's desire?
10. After you have made a choice about what you desire, what is the most important choice you have left?
11. Can you explain the difference between blind faith and understanding faith?
12. Can you explain why blind faith still has its place once you have developed understanding faith?
13. What opportunity often arises in a person's life when they are experiencing profound disappointment or a feeling of emptiness?

14. Explain the difference between Good Householder #1 and Good Householder #2.
15. What sets the attitude of Good Householder #2 apart from that of Good Householder #1?
16. What does the Real You use to grow your spirituality?
17. What does the much sought-after state called Enlightenment have to do with your essence?
18. What are the three tools necessary for accessing and bringing into expression your potential?
19. What do you call the part of you that watches the parade of thoughts and feelings as they pass through your mind without criticism or judgment?
20. What is it called when you disengage from the roles you play in life?
21. What are two other important actions that are a part of the answer to #20?
22. Why should you avoid mind candy?
23. What is the ninth step in the basic steps of meditation?
24. What happens to us spiritually when we are working hard to accomplish a goal through understanding faith?
25. According to Maurice Nicoll, what is the greatest obstacle to our spiritual growth?
26. Why do subpersonalities hang around after the need for them has been resolved?
27. Procrastination is not a cause but is rather a result of what?
28. Can you see ways in which you detour rather than change?

Developing A Fearless Attitude

29. The tension you create by striving to be perfect cuts you off from what?
30. When you have feelings of not being good enough, to what idea is your unhappiness connected?
31. What is the term for a motivated method of blocking something painful from our conscious awareness?
32. When you find yourself once again experiencing the same type of limiting relationships, jobs, etc., what is this called?
33. Why does the boomerang effect occur?
34. How do you define coping and why is it not a good approach to your life?
35. The path of least resistance has a double meaning. Explain the meaning that is not the path best chosen.
36. How do you combat your conditioning?
37. What are the five stages involved in harmonizing your subpersonalities?
38. Outside of efforts related to your mental and emotional natures, what is a physical effort that can jumpstart your self-esteem?
39. What are 7 ways to fire up your life?
40. Why does a person's purpose often center around outer works?
41. What is the importance of kinetic energy to your personal growth?
42. Explain what the false personality is.
43. Take a few minutes to review the 7 sure-fire ways to lose everything to make sure that you recognize the attitudes that can trip you up.

44. What are four things that can sway your state of mind, creating stress?
45. What is the real power behind your thoughts?
46. What are ways you can level the playing field when your emotions are dominating your actions?
47. What do you call the inherent drive within you to succeed?
48. In turn, what is the drive that is the tendency which causes forms to disintegrate or deteriorate to lower levels of organization, that is, to fall apart?
49. What is the one purpose that all problems serve?
50. What is the name of a technique you can use when confronted with resistance or confusing choices?
51. Why is it important to believe in divine restoration?
52. Why is it important for your life goals to satisfy a yearning within you?
53. Why do you sometimes achieve a goal without feeling like you've accomplished anything?
54. What are the seven steps of the creative process?
55. What is the principle called that is involved with attracting and harmonizing your desires?
56. Which step of our creative process unleashes all the possibilities within our desire?
57. Why is wisdom important in the manifesting of our desires?
58. Why is it detrimental to look over your shoulder, so to speak, at past regrets and perceived failures?

Developing A Fearless Attitude

59. Once you engage in the serious process of review and reinterpretation of your experiences, why can you never return to your previous level of understanding?

60. Too much structure in one's life can lead to what?

61. In looking to implement change, what are two elements that must be balanced in your plan of action to get the desired result?

62. What is an important item to remember for everyone, not just baby-boomers, in regard to technology and achievement of one's goal?

63. What is the cardinal benefit of de-cluttering one's life?

64. What are the four areas of work in building a foundation for a fearless attitude?

65. In healing oneself, it is necessary to address four areas, one of which is learning how to express oneself. What are the other three?

66. What are the three strategies for developing a fearless attitude?

PART TWO

TARGETING YOUR POTENTIAL

CREATIVE PROCESS

When most people speak of the creative process, they are referring to the dictionary definition of "the ability to produce something new through imaginative skill." This process fails to recognize that what we do in the outer is dependent on how well we work through the psychological barriers we have set up for ourselves.

When we speak of the Creative Process, we are referring to the method through which all creation came into manifestation. This process is a spiritual constant, and it is how we, as creative beings, create the lives we live. It is primarily a MENTAL process. It results in manifestation, but the procedure itself revolves around creating a *mental equivalent* of our desired goal, one that we can accept as true for ourselves. This acceptance determines the quality of our manifestation. It does not mean there is no outer activity, but the results depend on our mental state of mind.

We have mentioned our audio book several times before, and we bring it up again because it is built around the 7 steps of this Creative Process, which is constantly working in our lives whether we are aware we are using it or not.

YES, VIRGINIA, THERE IS A SYSTEM IN PLACE

(Note: The following was written as a special article request a few years ago to show why understanding the Creative Process matters.)

Yes, Virginia, there is a system in place that you cannot see that has brought to you all the things you've experienced in your life. That system is not controlled by others. It is controlled by you because it is your creative birthright.

Those who tell you otherwise are wrong. They have been affected by the belief that they are so small that nothing they do could possibly impact the Universe. They trap themselves into thinking small. So they only believe what they can see. Their minds are afraid to travel into the unknown to seek out answers.

To quote Francis Pharcellus Church from the New York Sun in 1897 in his famous response to Virginia: "there is a veil covering the unseen world which not the strongest man, nor even the united strength of all the strongest men that ever lived, could tear apart. Only faith, fancy, poetry, love, romance can push aside that curtain and view and picture the supernal beauty and glory beyond. Is it all real? Ah, VIRGINIA, in all this world there is nothing else as real and abiding."

Trusting in the Universe to provide through the systems that do exist — systems that are necessary to maintain the order that our scientists so diligently study — is the first step to experiencing a new life. The experiences in your life, whether good or bad, are being made manifest through the law of attraction. In talking about the law of attraction, you usually hear the simplified version of creation based on the Biblical verse "Ask and ye shall receive." A much more detailed version of this exists for you in the seven days of creation. The seven steps of this Creative Process define the way in which you are able to allow your desires to unfold in your life.

As a human being living your life, you cannot ignore that you are first a spiritual being. What does that mean for you? It means that being in this physical plane, you are not only dealing with the veil that exists between the Spiritual You living as a human and the non-physical or God — a veil that supports a belief in your separation from God — *but* you are also dealing with the erroneous ideas that you have accepted as being your reality.

These are ideas that you have heard others say about you or to you as you were growing up — ideas that reinforce your feelings of separation. When you accepted these ideas into your consciousness, they became part of the vibration that is YOU — in other words, the vibration that is attracting limiting experiences into your life.

The influence of the veil and these erroneous ideas is why it is so important, Virginia, to learn about the Creative Process, which is how you co-create. The acronym I created for keeping the steps of this process clear in my mind is as follows: *Processing Clarity Is Undeniably What Determines My Success* (polarity, commitment, imagination, understanding/will, discernment, mental equivalent, and the Sabbath). It not only helps in remembering the steps, but it underlines the key to achieving your desires—processing clarity in both your thoughts and your feelings from which manifestation emerges.

As you go through this season of new birth, Virginia, keep in mind that there is a system in place that is waiting for you to create the life you want to live.

Targeting Your Potential

QUIT THINKING ABOUT IT ... DO SOMETHING!

We've talked about the necessity for looking forward rather than looking back over your shoulder. Well, another thing to remember is that once you look forward, you have to do more than think about it!

Oh, I know, you want to make sure that you've thought it through before you do anything. I would say that's understandable — however, I have met way too many people who never get beyond thinking about it. I mean they don't even put their thoughts down on paper in any fashion, orderly or otherwise.

When I talk to people about the Creative Process, I explain to them that it is a mental process first and a physical process second. So, yes, you do have to think about what you want first. However, this does not mean that your desire is going to pop up in your space without your moving forward. Putting it on paper starts to take it from the metaphysical to the physical. It helps you during the time of your mental work to be able to imagine your ideas as a reality. It begins to take on shape and color in your mind.

Putting your ideas on paper takes you out of the comfort zone of your private thoughts. It helps you develop clarity about what you want. This is one of the primary reasons for preparing a business plan. It forces you to put your ideas down in black and white so that any flaws can be spotted. Otherwise, it's easy to "do a little sidestep" [Charles Durning] and set yourself up for failure.

The longer you wait to quit thinking about what you want and do something about it, the more resistance you will encounter within yourself. Refusing to take action, to commit yourself to your goal, gives all those "voices" of resistance within you more time to discourage you. Beat them to the punch by taking action: write your plan down, work it through, and start putting it into effect.

Targeting Your Potential

WHERE'S YOUR PASSION?

Do you have a passion for what you're doing? Do you feel great satisfaction every time you accomplish a project, finish a job, etc.? If so, you are on the right track. Hold tight to it.

Sometimes, however, you can fall victim to the demands of trying to *learn* everything and *do* everything. Then one day you wake up and wonder why this isn't as much fun as you thought it would be.

Does This Sound Familiar?

The message by popular internet marketing and business gurus is "outsource!" Unfortunately not everyone is in a position to hire people, virtual or otherwise. So you may feel stuck with doing all the aspects of your business. Everyone is telling you sure-fire ways to market your business. So, you spend a lot of time implementing them. You follow all the rules. Still, nothing seems to work. After a while, often years, you are in a state of burn-out. You can hardly motivate yourself to do another marketing strategy. You start to erase all the autoresponder emails that pour into your inbox every day without bothering to read them. You keep doing little things related to your business, but your heart just isn't in it anymore.

What's the answer? Do you quit? Do you keep plugging away at trying to get someone to notice you? You know your product is excellent. Everyone says so, but it doesn't seem to be enough. So, what is the answer?

What Is The Answer?

Get back to basics! Ask yourself: *what was the reason I started this in the first place? What was my passion? What was the thing I did that made me feel good?* I'm pretty sure you're going to realize that that's the ONE thing you're NOT doing anymore! That's what happened to me.

That's when I said to myself: Dannye, what makes you feel connected? What makes you feel good? My answer was "to write and teach." So that was when I decided that I was going to spend my time doing just that, and the great Internet Marketer in the sky would have to handle the rest of it.

The negative feelings I was generating within myself as a result of always doing something that didn't make me happy and NEVER having time to do the things that did make me smile were, I believe, affecting my marketing efforts and limiting my business. So, it was decision time. If I made the choice to do what made me feel good, it certainly couldn't diminish my current marketing results. If I started to feel good again, I would be generating *positive* feelings which could only enhance the vibration of myself and my business.

What Went Wrong?

The reality of all this is that the work I was doing **was NOT tied to my life intentions.** Becoming expert with dozens of software programs and implementing one marketing strategy after another was not fulfilling my heart's desire to be a writer and a teacher. That is why I was losing my enthusiasm. I wasn't in alignment with who I really am. Whether I ever achieve the long term goals I set for myself or not, I know now I'm going to enjoy the journey a lot more! I'll be more relaxed, happy, and fulfilled, which is what I was seeking in the first place.

So, if you're struggling, it's not necessarily a sign that you need to give up. Maybe your energy levels are waning because you are not in the flow of YOUR life. So rediscover your passion and make sure it takes center stage.

Targeting Your Potential

SELF-HELP PROGRAMS VS. THE CREATIVE PROCESS

Self-help programs are plentiful these days, especially with the advent of user-friendly publishing technology. So, you have access to more books, tapes, and seminars than you could ever have the time to absorb. Yet, even with those you choose carefully and religiously try to follow the steps they claim will take you to a specific result, you are faced with what you define as failure more often than not. Why is that? Why do you find yourself feeling discouraged, even depressed, by your inability to create positive change in your life?

What Do Self-help Programs Depend On?

To answer that question, let's talk first about *what is self-help*? Self-help covers a lot of topics. Some involve achieving a specific goal that is focused on money, relationships, or career. Such examples might be: *how to become a millionaire in one year – how to find your soul mate – how to obtain that coveted promotion*. Some involve personal growth or the ability to increase your understanding of yourself and your connection to the world around you. In other words, some center their attention on specific goals in the external world and others in your psychology.

Regardless of their focus, all of these programs have to abide by a system that is already in place. Whether you are a believer in God or science, all agree that there is an immutable order, a system that, thankfully, does not depend on our human input to function. Rather, it is the infrastructure, the underpinning, the support of all efforts that we as humans undertake.

The Cornerstone of the System

The cornerstone of this immutable system is a process that activates every time you have a desire of any kind. It is the process we have touched on briefly in this book, called the *Creative Process* because that is its basic function — to create or bring into manifestation whatever you desire. There are forces that govern the operation of this process, such as the Law of Attraction and the three forces of creation, which we have mentioned. When you activate a desire through your use of a self-help program, you are activating the Creative Process. So no matter what your goal or what steps your program outlines for you to reach that goal, **your desire will always follow the steps of the Creative Process and is subject to the forces that govern it.**

If you follow a self-help program, and it doesn't work for you even though you believe you followed all the steps that were outlined, would you be willing to consider that there must be another variable involved? Another influence on the final results? Understanding the environment in which all the self-help programs must function will assist you in being more consistent in reaching your goals.

The Critical Difference

You may ask at this point: What's the difference between the steps of a goal-oriented self-help program and the steps of the Creative Process? The answer is this: The steps of the goal-oriented self-help programs are only focused on outwardly achieving a specific goal. The steps of the Creative Process are focused on clarifying your thoughts and feelings so that you develop **the consciousness that will manifest the desired goal with consistency.**

Why does your consciousness matter? You can always force a goal into manifestation; however, the old saying — *What you have to fight to get, you have to fight to keep* — will determine your experience with it. The truth driving that statement is that unless you have the consciousness for a certain level of experience, it will not come easy to you. Being aware of the functioning of the Creative Process in everything you do and learning to work consciously with it will bring *permanent* change into your life. Rather than seeming like a closed loop, your life will gain direction and purpose.

Targeting Your Potential

So, if you want to transform your dreams from wishful thinking to reality, you need to make the effort to understand the system that is in place. Learn the rules of the process. Discover the ins and outs, the ups and downs that are inevitable but are simply part of the process for increasing your awareness of your potential as a "spiritual being having a human experience."

Make no mistake. It still requires hard work to master your life, to create the experiences you desire, but if you know the rules, you have a starting point and a direction. From there, you can develop the skills that make you a master of your own life — that enable you to process new knowledge and integrate it successfully into your experience.

7 Tips For Finding A Quality Self-help Program

Does your head start to buzz and your eyes start to cross every time you find yourself confronted with another self-help program? I don't blame you. So many people are on the self-help bandwagon that it has become too difficult and too time-consuming to separate the wheat from the chaff. Consequently, in the interest of sanity, you miss a lot of valuable resources because you toss everything into the trash.

Is there a solution? Yes, there is.

Every industry is full of those who talk in the abstract; that is, they don't really have a practical knowledge of what they're selling. Internet Marketing is a prime example. In my forays into this particular world in an attempt to educate myself, I encountered so many people who were only in it for the money. I can't tell you how many times I have signed up somewhere just to get a glimpse of what they offered only to discover that their sales pitch had more information in it than their product. After a few months of this, I was completely burned out and began a daily ritual of hitting the trash button every time I saw an email from some affiliate or internet marketer.

Is this the kind of experience you've been having with self-help books and programs? Have you tossed the baby out with the bath water rather than spend any more time trying to sort through the mass of products out there? If it is, let me share some ideas with you about what I consider the qualities of self-help programs that can make a difference.

Determining A Valued Resource

1. **Always presents information in a way that it has value for those who are seeking understanding but who have no background in the field, AND it also has value for those who have been involved in the field for a while.**

"For those who have eyes to see and ears to hear ..." This phrase means that I see and hear different things depending on where I am on my journey. If I read a particular book five years ago and thought it was great, but today my interpretation of the material is vastly different and it is still helpful, I am in possession of a valued resource. If I am able to see deeper layers to the work as I grow, it is indeed a valued resource!

2. **Discusses things in a practical way. In other words, it relates the information to situations that are common to a lot of people so that I can identify with it.**

If the body of a book or program is filled with grandiose examples or the writer/teacher spends most of the time citing cases of those who have been successful with their program, this is not useful information. Someone else's success is not my success. Their issues and their background are not necessarily the same as mine.

A valued resource gives me the "facts." It provides all the information I need to make decisions for myself so that I can address the beliefs and attitudes that are dominant in me.

3. **Does not use "catch phrases" with no attempt at explaining their significance.**

For example, the word "sin" has many connotations depending on the nature of a person's belief system. If I am to understand what they're saying, then I need to know how they define their terms. Do they define sin as a black mark on me or as a signal that I am off my path of well-being?

4. **Never tries to convince me that my success is just a matter of "doing" certain things.**

Doing things in the outer world, like making lists or following a particular regimen, is only one part of the process that effects permanent change in my life. The program should require that I

Targeting Your Potential

be willing to examine my thoughts and my feelings as well as my actions.

You run across some systems that focus almost exclusively on emulating successful people. Nothing wrong with that unless I never look at myself because I'm always looking at the focus of my attention. When that happens, my success, if it happens, is something I've forced into existence. It is not something for which I have developed the consciousness — in other words, something that grew out of my understanding. Consequently, it is on a shaky foundation.

5. **Encourages me to think for myself.**

   Any self-help program that discourages me from thinking for myself, that is, from tweaking what I've learned to understand myself is suspect. Growth is all about thinking creatively, and I can't very well do that if I take on the role of parrot!

6. **Never promotes itself as the only source of information for my personal growth.**

   If a self-help program or teacher expects me to accept only what they teach, their teachings are contrary to the underlying principal of personal growth. The underlying principal of personal growth is about my being creative — taking information I receive and embracing it, molding it until it takes me to a new level of experience. To do this, I must be free to explore all ideas that seem pertinent to me. I may choose to explore all the teachings of a particular source because they resonate with me. That's okay because I freely make the choice.

7. **Never assures me that my life will do a complete turn-around overnight.**

   Sure, my life is about change, but it is *life-long* change. It took a long time for me to develop the attitudes or beliefs that I currently hold. Most have become unconscious ways of looking at my life. Do you seriously think this is going to change overnight? Of course, I may be able to force a particular change near term, but the moment I take my attention from it, it will revert to the path of least resistance. So, even though I may have some new experiences right off, it is superficial. Real change comes from working on the underlying causes of my experiences, and that's a 24/7 job.

There are no quick fixes for my life or yours! Change is incremental, and anyone who tells me that they can permanently transform my entire life in a few quick and easy steps is totally ignoring 1) the work involved in change and 2) that my life is a journey of change through refinement.

Just as change takes time, so does making decisions about where to invest your energy in terms of your personal growth. Don't get discouraged or in too big of a hurry. Read about the people presenting the information. Make sure their desire is weighted toward wanting to help you rather than just making money.

There is *absolutely nothing wrong* with anyone making a living by helping other people. The difference lies in whether the money is a by-product of helping or the money is their primary motive for presenting the information. Of course, this is not so easy to determine sometimes. If they have a web site, check out their about us page. Google them. If they have podcasts or blogs, go there and check them out. Through all of this, you can get a feeling for the person(s). Trust your instincts!

Targeting Your Potential

VISIONS FOR LIFE AND BUSINESS

◉ Setting The Stage

HUMP? WHAT HUMP?

This question, asked by Igor in Mel Brook's *Young Frankenstein*, always seems to draw some of the biggest laughs by an audience. Why is that? Is it because Igor's hump is so obvious that we cannot imagine he would not know it was there, and we assume that he's being facetious? Although it is certainly successful as a laugh line, it carries with it deeper implications that affect us all.

If you are a business owner, you struggle to achieve the vision you have for your particular business, and it is not uncommon to find yourself disappointed with the results. You may assume that it's because you took a wrong action. You didn't advertise properly or you approached your customers in the wrong way. It is true that all these things have an impact on your business decisions; however, you can do everything right regarding financing, marketing, etc. but still fall short of your goal.

Goal setting, whether for business or personal, is a much described concept as well as an often misrepresented one. Achieving goals that you set for yourself is not strictly an outer activity. As I have mentioned, you can have all the support mechanisms in place for marketing, finance, personnel, and management and still fail to achieve your goals. Often you may be shocked to find that you achieved your goal but can't seem to sustain it.

Who's The Culprit?

The "Hump? What Hump? Syndrome" is responsible for many of our failures, ranging from personal relationships to full blown business ventures. The culprit is something which belongs to us by our very nature — ideas. Ideas are at the root of everything we do, and yet we continually underestimate the power that ideas we hold in mind have to produce the conditions in our lives. We ignore them the way Igor ignored his hump.

How is this possible? It's because we make the assumption that the only ideas that have power are those about which we are currently and consciously thinking.

Ideas are like seeds. If you plant a cantaloupe seed, you do not question for an instant that only a cantaloupe will come from it. Even if you forget about it, natural forces will nurture it with enough rain that it will likely be fruitful. It is only if you dig it up that it has no chance to produce the cantaloupe.

The same is true with ideas. If you have taken certain ideas into your psyche as a result of past experiences, low self-esteem, or others' expectations of you which are negative or failure-directed, simple goal-setting will not be successful.

These old attitudes, which are resistant to change, usually employ very subtle means of distracting you. How many times have you had an idea for improving your business but talked yourself out of it before you even gave it a chance? If you can think of a number of times, these old ideas of lack and limitation may have been around in your psyche for a long time.

You clothe and re-clothe them, justifying them with such names as "reality" or "too much competition" or "not enough time," etc. Once you recognize their existence, you'll wonder how you could have been harboring these beliefs for so long without realizing it. (Hump? What hump? Belief? What belief?)

How Do You Go About Ridding Yourself of These Sabotaging Elements?

1. You learn how to actively clothe an idea, that is, a chosen goal.

2. You practice analyzing your decisions to determine what influences were active in your final choices. This requires digging up those old seeds by being painfully honest with yourself.

Clothing an idea, that is, bringing that idea out of the abstract into the material, means you have to a) image it, b) embrace it with feeling, and c) act as if.

First, you have to see yourself experiencing the by-products of your goal: a fully booked appointment sheet, a store full of customers, your debts paid off—whatever it means to you. You have to image these things at least once a day, preferably more until you begin to experience feelings of excitement and anticipation when you think about them. When these ideas start to feel like a probability rather than a possibility, you will find yourself acting as if you have already achieved your goal, in other words, setting the stage.

As a result, you begin to implement actions which support the goals you have set, such as stepping out to buy that new software or piece of equipment, hiring the extra staff you have been needing, or committing to a marketing campaign.

The entrenchment of the "old timers"—those forgotten ideas—will not make it easy to manifest goals which are contrary to them. Consequently, you need to add a dash of time, persistence, and patience as you embrace your new ideas.

Make Sure Your Dream Doesn't Become A Nightmare

There are a lot of reasons why people choose to go into business for themselves. If you were to ask, some would tell you they didn't like the restrictions in the corporate world. Others would say they always felt at odds with everyone even though they were just trying to do a good job. But for whatever their reason, they struck out on their own . . .

- with the determination to put their ideas into practice in an environment where their ideas wouldn't be ignored or passed over for some idea far less innovative,

- with the determination to live in a world where risk of loss was not the issue, and petty jealousies were nearly unheard of.

Is this how you found yourself out there on your own? Did you also discover that there were elements in the process of bringing your ideas into manifestation that you had been taking for granted? Did you wake up a few months or even a year into your excellent adventure and long for a person to help you take care of the necessary, but uninspiring, work that was piling up on your desk and starting to invade your sleep?

This is the point when many small businesses crash and burn. It takes a lot of humility to admit that even those who aren't innovative serve a purpose in the workplace. It threatens your belief that corporate life is flawed. It can make you wonder if you made a mistake trying to make it on your own.

Are you one of these people? *Or* are you willing to admit that you misjudged the value of those you worked alongside in corporate who reliably took care of the day-to-day without trying to rock the boat? Are you willing to accept that you can't do everything yourself if you want to have time to transform your innovative ideas into reality?

Targeting Your Potential

You're in luck! Because there are so many people rushing into their own businesses today, other businesses are springing up to respond to this phenomenon. They are offering services to take the load off the frazzled small business entrepreneur. Some of these services have basic plans that are free. Services such as these keep you from having to buy expensive machinery or learn difficult software programs. There are also other professionals, such as virtual assistants, who can take the pressure off your day-to-day needs.

I don't know how often I've heard small business entrepreneurs say – *I feel like I spend all my time on the <u>business</u> of doing business. I never have time to develop my product or service the way I want to!* The need to take care of business is reality. In corporate, there were always other people assigned to take care of these things, and as an employee, you probably had the luxury of focusing your attention on one area. Now, most of you don't because you don't have the income yet to hire all those other people so you're having to do it yourself. That's why it's so important to look around and find services that are affordable, or better yet free, that can reduce your labor and your outlay of money. Yes, it does take a little time to find these opportunities, but that's why networking with other entrepreneurs is so valuable. This kind of information is easier to discover within these networking groups.

So once you start to get your approach to your business under control, and your head starts to clear, it's important to recognize that being a creative entrepreneur involves more than having a great product idea. It involves being creative about ways to ensure the quality of your life. Your life should not begin and end with your business.

When you are finally successful financially, what will you see when you look around you? Will you have any friends left? Or did they leave a long time ago because you were too busy for them?

Targeting Your Potential

What about family? Did they have to learn to tolerate your needs at the expense of their own? Or did they choose to leave, too?

What about you? Now that you've achieved this dream, are you having mixed feelings? Maybe you're happy but unclear about the future. Are you wondering what's next, afraid you can't top this performance and dreading the thought that the rest of your life will just be about maintaining your golden idea? Are you afraid of being dragged back to the humdrum life you ran away from in the first place?

The only answer to this dilemma is to *not* put all your eggs into one basket. Be creative. Just as you shouldn't try to do everything yourself in your business, you shouldn't allow your business to be the recipient of all your attention.

Learn how to balance your innovative, entrepreneurial side with the other areas of your life. Instead of taking time and energy from the success of your business, this effort will magically enhance your spiritual voltage, and every element of your life will burn brighter for it!

Develop The State Of Mind For Prosperity

Prosperity is dictionary defined as the "advance or gain of anything good or desirable." Most of the time when you think of prosperity, thoughts of financial, health, and social abundance arise. This is perfectly natural because we tend to define prosperity in terms of our worldly experiences. Often prosperity is equated with excesses of money, but prosperity is not about anything that can be quantified so easily.

You know that *thoughts are things*, which is shorthand for the creative processes you engage in every moment of your life. Consequently, it would seem that prosperity could be better defined by the **states of mind** that result in your outer abundance. In other words, attitudes such as, *being at one with who you are; being in the flow of Spirit; trusting; understanding the Law of Attraction; being full of joy!*

Achieving the Proper States of Mind

How do you achieve these states of mind? It happens over time through the work of change. Unfortunately, in our drive-thru society, people are often unwilling to invest the time necessary to develop the appropriate states of mind that will produce abundance in every endeavor. Instead, you follow some instructions, accomplish a near-term goal, and never look at anything beyond the manifestation. This approach is like tossing away the diamond ring your significant other gave you and falling in love with the box!

With a drive-thru mentality, every day is day #1 because your focus is outward on immediate gratification, not inward on building the necessary understanding for a lifetime of prosperity! You cannot expect to receive a magnificently served seven-course gourmet meal at a drive-thru!

Recall the attitudes I used to describe prosperity. What better describes your personal kingdom of heaven than *being at one with who you are; being in the flow of Spirit; trusting; understanding the Law of*

Attraction; being full of joy? Nothing! Once you accept that everything you could ever desire is a by-product of these states of mind, you are well on your way to achieving prosperity. However, that treasure trove comes to you over time through constant conscious attention to your thoughts and feelings.

You Must Apply What You Know

In the Bible, there is a parable that endeavors to describe an aspect of the kingdom of heaven through the story of a master who, after giving his three servants talents according to their abilities, went away. Each of his servants had the free-will choice of how to use those talents. These servants knew their master well. Two of the servants followed the guidance they had gained from their master and used their talents in ways that increased their prosperity. The third servant who received only one talent was afraid that despite the knowledge he received from his master, he would lose his talent. So he buried it in the ground.

When the master returned, all the third servant had to offer was the same talent which he had received. Calling him a wicked and slothful servant, the master instructed *"Take therefore the talent from him, and give it unto him which hath ten talents. For unto every one that hath shall be given, and he shall have abundance: but from him that hath not shall be taken away even that which he hath. And cast ye the unprofitable servant into outer darkness: there shall be weeping and gnashing of teeth."* (Matthew 25:28-30)

Knowledge of your connection to the Divine and of your creative inheritance cannot take you anywhere by itself. If you spend all your time reading books and going to classes and fail to practice *what you know*, you will be like the fearful servant who buried his talent in the ground. Not only will prosperity in all its forms *not* be your experience, but even that which you have will slip away. The parable declares that you will be cast into outer darkness. This means that as long as you are not applying the knowledge you

Targeting Your Potential

have gained in your life, you are living in darkness. You are denying yourself your creative inheritance. In other words, you have chosen a mechanical life.

Don't Let Fear Call the Shots

The third servant with only one talent was afraid, and fear can have no place in your creative process unless it alerts you to the fact that you are looking outward to the world as your source. Fear is your guidance system telling you that you have veered off course. Failing to heed this warning will short-circuit your efforts toward any goal.

The work of change means moving forward with courage. When your primary goal is to align yourself with who you really are, the work you do will reward you with new understanding and greater prosperity than you dreamed possible in whatever areas are important to you. *"Unto every one that hath [understanding] shall be given [greater understanding], and he shall have abundance."* The work of change *is* your kingdom of heaven.

When you desire to create abundance in your life, you have to choose to:

- consciously participate in the creative processes that continually unfold your life;
- willingly release your fears and embrace your creative nature;
- allow Spirit to flow freely through you by trusting in your oneness.

Understand that you are in this physical experience to create. Consciously participate in the process and apply what you know, and prosperity in all things desired is a given. The most desirable gain, however, will be in targeting your potential through your growth in consciousness. You will double the talents you were given by increasing your ability to be a Conscious Creator.

Targeting Your Potential

SKYROCKET THE IMPACT OF YOUR TALENT

When you have a talent, it is a gift from God. When you use that talent, it has the power to touch the lives of others. However, it is your personal vibration that determines how much energy the gift ultimately generates.

If you are caught up in your garbage or your negative conditioning (in other words, you are not accepting yourself unconditionally), your vibration limits how much energy is generated by the expression of your talent.

Say that you are a writer or a singer. You literally feel that you tap into the flow of Spirit when you write or sing. People are touched by your work. However, it doesn't seem to flow out into the Universe. People love it, but they don't pass it on. It goes just so far and stops.

Have you experienced this with your talent? A lot of us have. The reason these people don't pass it on is because the energy associated with your expression is not great enough. There's enough energy to touch them, but there doesn't seem to be enough left to encourage them to pass it on.

I look at this phenomenon in equation form. The level of energy associated with the expression of your talent can be expressed using these values:

- the expression itself is one value (Talent)
- how much you embrace who you really are and your talent is another value (YOU).

In other words, **YOU x Talent = The Level of Energy associated with your expression.**

The more you work to embrace who you really are rather than beating up on yourself or pretending to be someone you're not, *the greater the multiplying effect it has on your work.*

Just be confident in yourself. Know that you're okay. You're not perfect. No one is. You don't have to keep score against anyone else. There's no point because you're not trying to get into their flow of energy! You're trying to find your own.

Putting this in practical terms let's say you're a writer, then: YOU x Your Book = The Financial Success of your book.

If you feel good about yourself regardless of what anyone else may say or even regardless of the quality of your book, your work carries huge amounts of energy. *Now* when people read it, the excess of energy will have to be passed on to others! In the physical world, that translates into sales, which releases the energy of money to flow back to you!

REKINDLE YOUR PASSION

"Our life is frittered away by detail...Simplify, simplify."

- Henry David Thoreau

Sometimes we get so bogged down in details that we lose sight of our passions. The details overwhelm our resolve, and we slowly begin to mold ourselves and our business into the image others expect of us.

This is especially true for solopreneurs because it is usually a passion that started them on the solopreneur path in the first place. However, as I mentioned earlier, there is so much to learn to be competitive in today's technological world that it takes a lot of time and energy. Plus, there are so many people out there telling you in great detail exactly what you need to do to be financially successful.

Trying to be all of those people rolled into one can literally overwhelm you with details until you spend more time on *their* plan than on your own. Not only does your original passion often slip into the background, but it starts to mutate into something else. Instead of your passion driving your business — your business starts to be the driver, not your passion.

If you're feeling like your business isn't as much fun as you thought it would be or that the details of the business are completely sucking the life out of you, stop for just a minute. Take stock of your business. Are you doing what you started out wanting to do? Are you able to invest more energy in the creative side of your business related to your passion than you are in the "business" side of your business?

If your answer to these questions is "No," then you need to reassess. Unless your business is an expression of your passion, it will either become a j.o.b. or it will fail because you will lose your connection to it.

Targeting Your Potential

Every manifestation in life, including your business, has to spring from your thoughts and your feelings. Usually your business comes from thoughts and feelings that are incredibly strong — hence, your passion. So, as I said, if your connection with them starts to loosen, so will your connection to the goal your passion created.

My advice: Take a breath. Look at your business. If your passion is taking a back seat, invest some time and energy into figuring out how to reconfigure your business so that your passion is driving your business *or* consider the idea that there's something else you should be doing.

○ Leadership

DEALING WITH CRISES

What defines a crisis? Just mentioning that you're in a crisis can conjure up all sorts of negative or disaster-related thoughts and feelings for the listener. That's because we generally view a crisis as either irresolvable or as being catastrophic in its aftereffects – that is, leaving us damaged. A moment of rational thought, of course, can assure us that this is not always the truth. So what is it about a crisis that brings out such fear in people? This fear comes from feelings that emerge from ideas associated with a crisis. For example: obstacle, insurmountable, frustration, incapacitated, loss, failure — just to name a few.

In the workplace and in life, you have goals or plans. Seldom do you have total operational control over the unfolding of those goals in *either* environment, and yet you may still be the one with the dubious honor of saying, "the buck stops here." When this is the case, it is especially important for you to understand that a crisis is simply an event for which you must learn the necessary skills needed to resolve it efficiently.

What Are the Ways to Approach a Crisis?

How do most people deal with a crisis?

1. The *best* approach is to cope effectively and learn from the experience. Of course, this requires learning and using your crisis skills which we will be discussing later.

2. The *second* approach, which is quite common, is that of the survivor. The survivor has primarily learned to shut off his or her emotions and concentrate solely on the intellectual aspects of the situation. Tunnel vision serves to keep the survivor from

being side-tracked by the emotional force contained in those negative ideas we identify with a crisis.

A survivor actually appears to be quite competent to co-workers and family. However, the survivor is in a state of chronic crisis because he or she simply *ignores the feelings connected to any emotionally-elevated situation*. Consequently, these neglected emotions are always emerging at the most inopportune times!

3. The *third* approach is the person who simply falls apart in the face of upset. This person is incapable of dealing with any situation, either intellectually or emotionally, that is derailing the plan currently in place. Therefore, someone else has to step in and resolve the problems for him or her.

4. The *fourth* approach is quite common these days. All of us can recount experiences dealing with customer service representatives or co-workers who, in the face of being challenged, immediately employ the CYA approach. In laymen's terms, this is the "cover your ass" approach.

There are different strategies employed by adherents of CYA. One is to blame someone else, which leaves you clear of the fallout from the crisis. The other is play the role of a robot by repeating a set monologue over and over regardless of the input from other parties. The goal here is to try to appear that you are doing your job while hoping that eventually everyone will get frustrated and leave you alone.

Psychological and Environmental Influences

There are many psychological and environmental influences that determine how an individual responds to a crisis. In the workplace, powerful persuaders include: 1) the level of initiative allowed by the immediate supervisor and 2) the prevailing attitude of the employer regarding the outcome of previous crises. Often, however, the first consideration by an employee is the degree of responsibility he has for the ultimate outcome. Playing it safe is not unusual.

The workplace environment is not the only source for factors influencing the reactions of an employee. Your physical and emotional well-being that day is probably more significant in determining your initial reaction than anything else. Did you have an argument with your spouse that morning? Was yesterday bill-paying day? Is your car in the shop and no one will tell you how much it's going to cost? All of these things set a mood, and **that mood can be your starting line for whatever comes your way that day**, including the crisis.

Lifelong patterns established from family relationships also transfer to workplace relationships. If you have developed patterns of behavior in your private life that do not support assertiveness and taking the initiative, it is not likely you will be able to act out differently at work.

Skills Needed By Managers and Employees

Because of the variables that affect each of us every moment of the day, it is necessary to learn the skills for dealing with a crisis. Learning a skill means developing a new pattern that can bring a situation to a successful conclusion. If you are a manager, you will have your own share of crises, but you must also learn how to be skilled as a advisor in a crisis so that you can help your employees learn to cope effectively.

As an unofficial counselor, a manager should:

- Develop a rational and stable environment in order to restore a sense of balance for the employee. Curses, threats, blame, or condemnation do not serve any purpose.
- Use the experiences that have made you a manager to initiate creative thinking so that you can serve as a resource for your employees.

- Be creative and open-minded. Do not rigidly try to apply an old fix to a new problem. Listen to what your employees are telling you. They are usually closer to the details.

- Believe in the abilities of your employees, but recognize individual differences. You have to know the strengths and weaknesses of all your employees. This enables you to bring just the right people in to work on the problem if necessary.

- Take it one step at a time and give yourself time to think things through. In other words, do not panic.

- Make sure that you arrange your workload so that there is enough energy allotted to "managing." If you have allowed the production side of your job to overwhelm the management side of your job, dealing with a crisis appropriately is going to require more energy than necessary. Why? Because you're going to be busy playing a game of "catch-up."

- Be willing to consult with your own supervisor if you get in over your head. Everyone, even an owner, has someone to whom they can look for advice. Brainstorming is a powerful tool. Use it.

As an employee, it is important that you assess the situation in light of what you know. Just like your manager, you need to be creative and open-minded to new ways of looking at the problem. Can you handle the situation by yourself? If so, then do it. However, don't be afraid to seek out answers to things you don't know from your co-workers or your supervisor before the crisis escalates. Most important, don't try to hide a crisis. It won't go away.

The Best Approach to Any Crisis

Dealing with a crisis is easier if you have a step-by-step process to use. It serves the same purpose as the automatic pilot mechanism in an airplane. It continually brings you back to your heading if you start to drift off course. So, let's examine that process.

Targeting Your Potential

Step 1. Define the problem.

Step 2. Determine what the immediate danger is and if it can be temporarily halted until a solution is found.

Step 3. Get feedback from co-workers, supervisors, peers, etc. if needed.

Step 4. Examine your alternatives.

Step 5. Make a plan for dealing with the crisis.

Step 6. Get approval from anyone whose cooperation you will need.

Step 7. Act.

Step 8. Reassess the situation to determine if it is fully resolved.

Step 9. Make notes — mental or otherwise — that will be beneficial for the future.

The intensity of any crisis can only be measured on an individual level because each of us has different skill levels. Engaging problems through the use of the nine-step process above adds to your reservoir of knowledge and increases your skills for dealing with future problems in the workplace and in your life.

One final note: In the workplace the most popular usage of the term crisis is in conjunction with the phrase *crisis management*. However, crisis management is a disease of the procrastinating manager and the thrill junkie. A crisis, on the other hand, is simply an occurrence that can strike anyone, anywhere, anytime. A crisis is an event which tests our mettle and can enrich our personal growth.

Is Your Business Partnership Working?

Partnerships are an interesting experiment. They can be a wondrous experience, joining two harmonious individuals who work together for the sake of a common goal. However, a partnership can simply be an opportunity for you to make conscious decisions that can change the flow of your life.

If a partnership isn't working for you, what you find yourself experiencing is usually anger, fear, upset, name-calling, or any number of other negative emotions. This is also known as resistance. Resistance is a natural phenomenon, so it does serve a purpose. It is part of what provides you with choices.

Goal-focused Partner

When you entered the partnership, you may have expected that wondrous experience I described. Instead, resistance entered the picture. You and your partner seem to be at odds. Perhaps you are actually trying to focus on the goal while the other is more focused on their ego-driven needs: not a healthy relationship, one that will surely lead to discord. Over time, as the more goal-focused partner, you become frustrated by the copious amounts of energy required to pick your way around the ego-driven landmines along the way, and you start to lose your focus on the original goal.

So, what do you do now? Do you keep giving in to the thrusts and jabs, making yourself even more miserable or do you walk away? A difficult question to answer sometimes, and you can't really answer it until you allow yourself time to get past the negative emotions that have been stirred up. Without attention, negative emotions will languish. Give yourself time to let them fade away. *Then make your decision about staying or leaving the partnership based on what is best for you.*

If this partnership is a repeat of other relationships in your past — relationships that have not been satisfying — then why should you consciously choose to remain in this one? You cannot change your state of being by beating the resistance into a bloody pulp. You change by recognizing what is before you and making a conscious decision to not participate in such a relationship. However, your decision has to be made *after* you are in a state of non-resistance, a place where the negative emotions have faded away.

The resistance, the actions of your ego-driven partner, have taken you to a place of decision. Now it is up to you to apply the conciliatory force of *conscious thought*, free of negativity, or to apply the conciliatory force of *tit-for-tat* to the partnership situation, effectively increasing the power of the resistance. Choices. They are yours to make.

Ego-driven Partner

On the other hand, if you are the ego-driven partner, you may be finding this partnership a tasty fare indeed. The battle for supremacy is a negative enterprise. Consequently, increased resistance only heightens the excitement for you. If your partner's choice is to apply tit-for-tat, you will probably consider yourself a winner — mostly because the partnership is not about the business goal for you. It is about your ego needs, and the match is just getting interesting.

However, life does not offer its lessons to one and not the other. You, too, have the opportunity to make choices here that can change your state of being. Because of the appeal of the negativity in the partnership, you probably won't notice this opportunity unless your partner chooses to walk away. Then, deprived of sustenance, you are given the opportunity for a conscious shock, a moment in time to see yourself clearly. You can make the choice to continue allowing your need for control and worldly validation to dominate your actions or you can choose another path. Choices. Again, they are yours to make.

Are Partnerships Always A Crapshoot?

Partnerships *can* be wondrous experiences. It's just that life offers us opportunities to learn, to grow, and these opportunities usually involve interactions with other people. Partnerships happen to fall into that category. Not all partnerships have such potent lessons attached to them. Some simply provide smaller lessons along the way.

Whatever your experience is or has been, remember these things first:

1. There is value to be found in every negative experience.
2. You must give your negative emotions time to fade away before you make a decision.
3. Allow yourself to be in the moment, fully conscious.
4. Then apply the conciliatory force of conscious thought, free of negativity, to the situation and do what feels right for you.

Although this chapter has focused on business partnerships, everything here applies to personal relationships as well. Every healthy relationship demands that people are able to work well together, and every relationship is the basis for life lessons.

Ethics: Do They Matter?

What do you do when no one's looking? Several answers probably popped into your mind. We've all caught ourselves doing things when no one was looking that we might not dream of doing otherwise.

What came to your mind? Maybe taking a few office supplies home with you from work? Not telling the clerk he didn't ring up everything he sacked? These things are not unusual, and most, if asked, would rate them benign. Yet, the question of ethics is a hot topic in today's world. I hear speakers addressing ethics from all angles: ethical leadership, ethical social behavior, ethics in the workplace, and so on. *Why is there such an interest in ethics and ethical behavior?*

Ethics

By dictionary definition, ethics has to do with our moral principles or values. What exactly does this mean? Is it talking about what you say you would do under certain conditions? If given hypothetical situations, most people say they would do the "right" thing. However, the true barometer of one's values is found in crises, not in answers to questions about speculative situations. The looting which has taken place during riots occurring in this country in the last fifty years speaks loudly of the values of those involved. The acts of kindness you have seen during crises resulting from hurricanes and tornadoes and other weather disasters also reflect the true values of those involved.

What you do — good or bad — when your actions are not subject to review or consequences comes nearer reflecting your true values than anything else you do. If you don't steal or lie or cheat, etc. because there are laws against it or because you might get caught, then your behavior is not truly ethical behavior. *It mimics ethical behavior but is not cut from the same cloth.*

For your life to reflect these moral principles or values, you must continually assess your actions toward others, toward your commitments to others, and toward their property. You're probably thinking, *that's a principle easier said than done*, but there are ways to check yourself on a daily basis.

- You can start by putting yourself in the other person's shoes. Ask: *"Would I appreciate my actions if I were on the receiving end? Would I feel hurt or angry or cheated or betrayed?"*

Stepping outside your private world and imagining someone else's is a first step in building the foundation for ethical behavior. Doing what is moral or right, doing what harms no other, requires that you have some notion of what another person experiences.

Empathy. Without it, you make "intellectual" decisions about situations and those involved in them. Such decisions are rarely based on actual facts. Instead, they are based on beliefs you have adopted to support the ideas you are emotionally able to accept.

Buffers

To protect these beliefs, in truth to hide their flaws from yourself, you develop what are called *buffers*. For example, our original illustration of a person not letting a clerk know they failed to ring up everything on the register is usually justified by a moral balancing act. You contend that the store overcharges anyway, and this just helps to balance the scales a little. *So what if their profit margin is a few bucks less?* This reasoning is simply a buffer.

You might insist, if confronted, that it's not your fault the clerk is incompetent. True, you didn't hide the item from the clerk, but you are aware that you didn't pay for it. That makes you guilty of knowingly taking the item without paying for it. In a court of law, that makes you guilty of shoplifting.

What position does this put you in? What was your reaction the last time you heard about some person in the community or some celebrity being caught shoplifting? Probably you shook your head slowly, summoning up your most pious expression, and expressed your total inability to understand why anyone would do such a thing.

If you were to admit to yourself that you were guilty of the same offense, despite the fact that the clerk's negligence initiated the act, you would not be able to reconcile the attitudes you use with others. It would break down the fragile foundation of what you believe about the world you live in, including your place in it. The buffer shields you from the truth, packaging the event so that you are emotionally able to accept it. Buffers protect you from your inconsistencies..

Often these buffers serve to keep your fears at bay. If pushed to the wall, many people find themselves questioning their beliefs whether these are psychological, religious, political, or social beliefs. It is not common for people to have beliefs born out of a truly balanced perspective. You are skewed by your experiences, your families, your fears. Things people don't understand are often labeled as morally wrong when it has nothing to do with morality. Rather it has everything to do with whether it fits into their personal belief systems.

Our Skewed Perspectives

You can see this very clearly on a broader, cultural level, especially in today's dynamic climate. *Ethnocentrism* is the tendency to use one's own cultural values to judge the behavior and beliefs of people raised in other cultures.

In cultures possessing strong religious bases that also drive their political agendas, it is improbable that they can practice such ethnocentrism *and still interact harmoniously* with cultures whose religious bases are different. Usually, their strong need to be right excludes the possibility of others' being right as well.

Although many believe that you should not judge or interfere in the cultures of others, intervention in circumstances such as Nazi Germany are justifiable for distinct reasons: 1) the persecuted within that culture actively sought help from *outside*; 2) those in control within that culture tried to *impose their beliefs on those in other cultures as well.*

If the person's actions being judged are not infringing on your freedom to act in a way you consider acceptable, if you are not being physically harmed in any way, if a third party is not seeking help to be freed, and if your property is not being damaged by their actions, then by what moral right do you assume that their actions should be changed or curtailed by you? Yet, we as individuals and nations do this every day.

Politicians are famous for declaring a moral platform when it suits them. Unfortunately, the moral platform is used to manipulate people and situations and validate actions by not only politicians and religious leaders, but *also by you and me.*

Our first foothold out of this rut in which we find ourselves is by **being aware** that we tend to view the world with not only an *ethno*centric, but also an *ego*centric eye and then by **endeavoring** to open our minds and hearts to another's view.

You're probably wondering how this relates to your personal life. Your workplace, your neighborhood, your family, and even strangers on the street are judged by you according to what your egocentric view considers to be acceptable behavior. Everyone does this at one time or another. You might also ask yourself how many times you have tried to impose your views on your co-workers or family with no concern for their beliefs because you believed your perspective was the right one.

What Goes Around Comes Around

- Next, ask: *"Would I act this way if I knew, without a shadow of a doubt, that the same action would be inflicted on me in the future by someone else?"* Does this make you think twice about taking advantage of another? The old adage "What goes around comes around!" does have truth in it.

Whether or not you are willing to admit it to yourself right now, the truth remains that what you send out into your environment, your universe, will find its way back to you in some form. It is seldom that those you injure psychologically, physically, or financially are the source of your comeuppance. Instead you will find yourself being injured in some way by someone not unlike yourself.

Usually when it happens to you, you never relate it to your own past actions. You generally feel you are undeserving of such adversity. You embrace the same feelings of hurt, anger, or frustration that earlier victims of your unethical behavior may have felt. The narrowness of your view is a result of your self-centeredness, which makes the upward slope toward change even more slippery.

- Another test of ethical behavior involves asking yourself: *"Am I living up to my commitments?"* If you goof off in your job or create dissension among co-workers or inject negative energy into the work environment in any way, you are not living up to the commitment you made when you were hired. This is not ethical behavior.

Commitments are not limited to the workplace. We each have commitments within the family structure. It can be as simple as chores and as complex as your role within the family dynamic. Whatever the particulars, the function of the whole — work or family — depends upon your honoring your commitments.

Do your children do their chores without your having to remind them or look over their shoulders? If not, you are not teaching them the importance of commitment, or perhaps you are not setting the right examples. If you make up stories to take time off from work or go in late, you are affirming for them that unethical behavior is okay. If you talk about your employer or friends in derogatory terms behind their backs, you are undermining any other efforts you make to verbally teach your children right from wrong.

Such actions teach them that commitment to relationships and promises only matters when they are the beneficiaries. Otherwise, it can be tossed aside. In the previous question, we noted that "what goes around, comes around." This is just as true here. If everyone adopts this attitude toward commitments, then you are bound to be the recipient of irresponsible actions by another.

Me First

This *Me First* attitude has been prevalent for a long time. This attitude mimics a sociopath or a person with Antisocial Personality Disorder. According to the Diagnostic and Statistical Manual of Mental Disorders, a sociopath has a *"pervasive pattern of disregard for, and violation of, the rights of others"* with *"deceit and manipulation"* as chief features. He tends to be *"consistently and extremely irresponsible."* A sociopath *"frequently lacks empathy."*

Recognize any of these symptoms from our discussion so far? Curb the extreme nature of the pathological condition called Antisocial Personality Disorder, and you would have a **Me First** person. The "Me First" will probably never be defined as a mental disorder for clinical determination. However, it can have just as many risks for the individual and others as those associated with bona fide Mental Disorders.

Fear by some religious and political groups has resulted in people unfortunately applying this same label to philosophies which do not deserve it. Those people today who are struggling to change their lives by working on themselves and refusing to participate in activities and relationships which are spiritually and emotionally damaging are often labeled as advocates of "Me First." It is insinuated they have all the characteristics we outlined as sociopathic.

In reality, these persons are *not* being irresponsible as is inherent in the "Me First" philosophy. These individuals understand certain axioms:

- They can only change themselves.
- They cannot force their beliefs on anyone else.
- Only by changing themselves can they have an impact on the Universe.

The accusations hurled at these people have fears underlying them which are actually the buffers of those doing the accusing. The fear may be either ignorance or a fear of change. Whatever its cause, fear, especially when joined with others of like mind, will seek to control or discredit those who think differently.

- *"Am I experiencing gain at the expense of another?"* We cannot maintain the energy required to sustain a position or status we "stole" from another. It is not a universal law that there must be a loser if there is to be a winner. We must earn our own place.

My stepson told me about a body builder who used constant taunting to undermine the confidence of another body builder so that he could take away his title. It seems the title holder had a physical impairment but had refused to allow it to hold him back. However, his determination was not prepared for the cruel taunting of the contender. He lost.

In my stepson's eyes, the contender was *never* a winner. Even today, years later, he cannot let go of the image that this man "stole" his title. Some would say that it's all part of the game, but that's just because we allow it to be. Body building is supposed to be about form and mass, not manipulation. Moral behavior is just as important in sports as it in our daily lives.

Manipulation and Lies

Using manipulation or deceit to gain a promotion over a co-worker affects those around you and yourself. If those you now manage, for example, feel that you connived to get promoted, you will never be able to draw the best from them because you set the stage with your own unethical behavior.

A child lying about who was responsible for breaking a vase can set the stage for continued unethical behavior as an adult. Often, parents assume that one child is guilty over another without actually listening just because of the relationship they have with one of them. This is irresponsible. It may validate the behavior of the lying child and affirm for the victim that morality has no value.

- Finally, ***"Do I judge the rightness or wrongness of my action by whether anyone knows about the act?"*** This is the very essence of ethics. It isn't about what we do or who knows about it. It is about who we are, which means that we would act the same whether we were alone or in front of a TV camera with millions of people watching.

Do you choose your actions based on the benefits you can get from others? Do you return the shopping cart to the cart rack? Do you pick up an item off the floor at the store and put it back on the rack or the shelf, or do you just walk around it? Do you put your cigarette butts in the ashtray or throw them out the car window? These are all actions which are probably not going to be noticed by anyone. How often do you make the responsible choice?

Would you give a large sum of money to a charity anonymously or would you want others to know? Would you go to the store and buy groceries and just leave them on the doorstep of someone who was desperately in need? How hard is it to be anonymous when you do a good deed? If you can't, perhaps you should question your motives.

Conclusion

In the discussion of these five points, we can see that unethical behavior can affect every aspect of your life. You may wonder, however, why there is now such an interest in ethics and ethical behavior.

I believe it is because we as humans are in the throes of change, and the motivating force behind that change is Love. This is not love as most of us define it. This Love is cosmic. It is vast. It is the cosmogonic spark which ignited the Universe.

If we can learn to use the energy of this cosmic Love to function, we will always seek to do that which does not harm any other, and that is what ethical behavior is — behavior expressed from Love!

Your View Of Your Business Sets Its Tone

Whether you're encountering a problem or an opportunity in your life, ask yourself "*What is my point of observation?*" Let's say, for example, you own a business called Books I Love to Read, and you are in dire need of information on how to market on the internet. Synchronistically, a fellow networker tells you about a free seminar that is reportedly about internet marketing. *Great! This is exactly what I need,* you think to yourself.

However, when you get there, you are bombarded by the agenda of the seminar sponsor. Although you really just wanted to acquire a direction or some sources for implementing a viable marketing program for your business online, you find yourself getting caught in the swell of sales gimmicks. The promise of help in learning to market on the internet was just a way to draw you in.

If you're not careful, however, your **point of observation** will shift away from that of a person whose passion is to attract booklovers and sell them books they'll love to read. You will wake up and find yourself reaching for a different goal — a goal that matches the needs of the seminar sponsor. Suddenly your point of observation is *now* about being a web tycoon. You're ready to sell anything that will fit the model they have laid out for you. It doesn't even matter if it has anything to do with books. Now it's all about *money!*

When you set yourself a personal goal for your business, or your life for that matter, you should set out what your intention is and measure every decision against that intent.

In the example, your intention for your business might be that you want to use your passion for reading to develop a business where you can not only share your passion, but make money doing it. If you always measure your decisions against that intent, what does this mean? It means that it is perfectly okay to explore opportunities if they appear to offer elements that will enhance your original intent.

In my example, you did need to know more about internet marketing. However, you have to be discerning enough that you *don't let others distract you from your intent*. Listen to the information, do your research, measure what you find against your stated objective for your business, and then make a decision.

I believe most people fail in business because they lose perspective. They start viewing their business through the eyes of other people.

If your business is your *heartsong*, it doesn't matter if you fit the patterns established by others or not, you can still be a success. In the movie *Happy Feet,* Mumble had his own unique heartsong, and so do you. As long as you make sure that your **point of observation remains connected to your Intent** for your business, you will move steadily forward on your path to success!

CREATE GOALS THAT LEAD TO SUCCESS

Whether in life or business, you have to take action to avoid mistakes that could be fatal to your success.

Create a vision for both near term and long term goals.

It's okay to say you want to be a multi-millionaire. It's a goal, and one that's exciting to think about, but for most people, going from perhaps $30,000 a year to $1,000,000 needs to be broken down into bite size pieces.

Think about a nice, juicy 16 oz. steak. If you're a vegetarian, think about a nice, scrumptious vegetable casserole dish. Can you imagine yourself eating that entire steak in one bite? Or gulping down the casserole in one bite? Of course not! You can eventually eat the whole thing, but it requires a process of one bite at a time.

Life is like that. When you create a goal, you have to be able to accept it as being realistic so that your emotional nature can get involved in the process. The long term goal of being a multi-millionaire can seem more like wishful thinking, which will never take you there. However, when you break this goal down into bite size pieces, you find it easy to get excited about each piece, and before you know it, you've achieved your long term goal!

For example, Let's say that you produce a number of products, such as books. By focusing on goals for individual product sales over a year's time, you are able to break it down so that you start to see how your long term goal can become a reality.

It's easier to see yourself selling 200 books a month than 5000 books a month. Once you've made it through the first year with this approach, however, the goals you set for the following year will be different because you now have a different sense of yourself and your business. You have discovered that the experience of the last year has given you greater confidence. Consequently, your ability to imagine being a multi-millionaire is increasing. The goals you set for your second year will be much more assertive.

So, be sure that you have a long term goal even if it is one that you would be embarrassed to share with anyone else in the beginning. Just make sure that you create short term goals all along the way. Some people create 5, 10, and 15 year goals. I believe, however, that most of us need to break it down into smaller pieces, or we're likely to choke on it.

My advice: Take bites that are manageable for you. Take the time to chew. Don't rush to swallow so that you can move on to dessert. Allow yourself to savor the experiences. You will learn a lot more about yourself and your business this way. You may even find that dessert tastes better when it finally does arrive!

EVALUATE YOUR BUSINESS FOR SUCCESS

My book titled *The 12-Step Business Plan for the Solopreneur* helps you achieve a clearer vision of the elements affecting your success. Once you have reached this place, it is time for you to create a graphic analysis of your Strengths, your Weaknesses, Your Opportunities, and the Threats to your success.

I suggest that you actually label four sheets of paper, one for each characteristic.

Strengths   Weaknesses   Opportunities   Threats

You'll need to be honest. Don't hold back. If you have a partner or a mentor, brainstorm with them. Don't try to do it at one sitting. Keep it handy and when something occurs to you, write it down. You'll be amazed at what develops!

Using the SWOT Analysis

When you use the SWOT Analysis to assess your business vision, you have to know the answers to a series of specific questions:

1. What am I selling?
2. How am I selling it?
3. To whom am I selling it?
4. How does it reach them?
5. What are the investments, costs, and prices?
6. How do I manage all this?

So I suggest you think about the answers to these questions first.

***It is important to note that the SWOT Analysis is not a one-time exercise. This can be done when launching a new product or a new division — any time you need to clarify your position before taking a new or different path.

Use your sheets of paper to answer the questions below and any others that may come to mind.

Strengths

This should be a listing of strengths you believe give you the edge over your competition. If you're just starting out in business, you probably don't have a reputation to protect. You may not even have a strong brand developed. However, don't despair! You still have strengths.

If your business is based on a solid idea, then the strengths are inherent in your idea. These questions can get you started:

1. Why do I think my product/service will benefit the consumer more than what is already available?
2. What expertise do I have that adds credibility to my business?
3. What do I do well in terms of sales, marketing, management, etc.?
4. Is there a special element to my business that gives me an advantage over the competition, such as a new perspective on an existing methodology?
5. Is my product competitively priced? [If not, this could be a weakness depending on how you market yourself.]

Continue on exploring the strengths of your business until you are satisfied.

Weaknesses

First, go back and look over your strengths to see if there is a weak area in any of them, i.e., something you haven't let yourself look at carefully enough.

Targeting Your Potential

Below are some questions to get you started.

1. Have I not developed a good branding strategy?
2. Do I have inadequate financial backing to purchase the products and/or services I need to operate my business?
3. Does my web site lack a shopping cart and/or the capability of building a list?
4. What other elements are missing that I deem necessary to succeed?
5. Have I not established a means for distributing my product/service?
6. Am I having trouble locating acceptable vendors or staff with which to work?

Opportunities

What are some opportunities that exist "out there" that can spell profit and growth for your business?

1. Did something change in terms of economic conditions, regulations, trends, etc. that will cause my product or service to be in demand?
2. Does my niche open up a frontier in my field?
3. Is there an untapped market for my product or service?
4. Are there market needs that I can target that aren't being met by my competitors?
5. Do I have new marketing strategies planned that will increase conversion rates (from site or location visitors to customers) for my product/service?
6. What connections do I have with others that can grow my business?

Threats

Threats are situations that occur outside your business that could threaten your current plan of action.

1. Does the industry itself have a negative reputation with the target market?
2. Do I have high-profile competitors who can easily underprice my product/service?
3. Does the market demand for my product/service tend to be seasonal?
4. Is there legislation that could impact my business vision?
5. Will I have difficulty retaining the skilled staff I need?
6. What obstacles do I know that I face?

Benefits

The benefits of a SWOT analysis can be ascertained through the use of a Matrix. So, it is time to take your 4 sheets of paper and place them in the arrangement of the matrix below where it is labeled Strength, Weaknesses, Opportunities, and Threats. Now, get 4 new sheets of paper and label them S-O, w-O, S-t, and w-t. These are the sheets of paper on which you will develop strategies.

	Strengths	Weaknesses
Opportunities	S-O	w-O
Threats	S-t	w-t

Through this process of SWOT Analysis, you want to *minimize* your Weaknesses and Threats and *maximize* your Strengths and Opportunities. Once you have determined what each of these are for your business, you need to determine the inter-relationships that exist between them.

Looking at the matrix above, you can see that when you consider **your strengths and your opportunities (S-O)**, you will be able to easily work out a strategy that will be profitable for your business.

With **your strengths and your threats (S-t)**, you are able to use your strengths as the basis for developing operational and marketing strategies that will defuse the threats to your business.

With **your weaknesses and your opportunities (w-O)**, you get a chance to apply Conscious Shock to your business. You get a chance to look at your weaknesses and see how you are able to step outside your comfort zone, turn a weakness into a strength, and take advantage of an opportunity.

With **your weaknesses and your threats (w-t)**, a great deal of problem-solving and brainstorming will have to take place to turn these around to your advantage. However, the energy invested here only makes your business stronger!

Each of your 4 new sheets of paper should eventually reveal a strategy that you have developed for making each inter-relationship an asset.

THE SUCCESS SPIRAL

When success is the topic of conversation, you will almost certainly hear someone utter words to this effect: "Find someone who is successful and emulate them." Of course, *emulate* implies that you are striving to surpass their efforts. Not bad advice if you're trying to change careers, but in the everyday world as we move from one task to another, it is not always possible or necessary to look for someone else to emulate. You can look to your own experiences as well. After all, you have been successful, too. It is unlikely that you have lived this long and not learned a thing or two, and learning is a hallmark of success.

So, let's review the steps that led to your success. You may not have described them quite like this, but you will recognize the process.

Step 1: Decide on a Direction

When action is required in any circumstance, a **decision** must be made about a choice of direction. This decision is based on past experiences, i.e., what you have learned from those experiences. You determine your direction by weighing the outcomes of prior choices and selecting the most successful one, hoping to improve on your earlier mistakes. *This decision establishes the task at hand.*

Once the task is settled, it is necessary to move forward in an orderly manner through steps which build the necessary foundation for its success. Together these steps forms a single level in what I call the **SUCCESS SPIRAL**. Each step leads to the success of the current task. The completion of each task takes us to the end of one level of the Success Spiral, creating the foundation for even greater success in future ventures.

Step 2: Planning and Preparation

The next step involves **planning**. It is impossible to be consistently successful without proper planning. You must determine the outcome you desire and the steps you will need to take to get there.

Once you have mapped out your course, it is imperative that the **preparations** involved in each step of your plan are outlined. Then a realistic scheduling of your time (and others') is necessary. This provides a framework within which to operate. Step two lays the groundwork or outlines the preparations.

Step 3: Performance

Step 2 cannot always be completed before some **performance** of the task takes place. You may have to toggle between preparation and performance as you work your way through the plan. This is not uncommon with complex tasks. Besides, it is not always possible to anticipate everything, and you may have to tweak your plan a bit.

Step 4: Controls

Performance of the task must be subject to certain **controls**. These controls are the elements which narrow the field of variables which could negatively impact your project. Obviously, expenditures and budget are prime variables. In addition, deadlines, quality levels, and a clear vision of the outcome will keep you (and others) on track.

Step 5: Coordination

Coordination of all the steps and all the persons involved contributes to a smooth operation. It is similar to "seeing the big picture." Keeping in mind where you are going and where you have been is enhanced by the level of controls in place. The coordinating process results in invaluable records.

Step 6: Records

The **records** of what has happened at every step of the plan are a priceless legacy to your future success. They should be thorough and objective. This is especially true if it is a group project. If it is a personal task, you may still want to jot notes in your day book or diary.

Step 7: Evaluation

The next step of the Success Spiral involves the **evaluation** of your efforts. This, too, should be objective. You need to view these records with a critical eye. Never fall into the trap of self-justifying your actions.

Once you have honestly evaluated all the steps and elements of this task and the performance of yourself and others, you should study your conclusions so that you retain what is valuable. In other words, store away for future use the lessons you learned, your conclusions, new techniques developed, etc.

Step 8: Feedback

Finally, record **feedback** from all those involved in the project and those affected by the project. Don't forget yourself! The feedback completes this level of the spiral.

With the knowledge and understanding you gain from this orderly process, you will be able to proceed upward on the Success Spiral. You will begin again by making a **decision** about your direction [goal] just as you did before, but your experience will be different if you completed the previous level.

If you failed to complete the process, if you did not evaluate yourself and the operation honestly, you will not learn anything. There's a reason for the saying: "Insanity is doing the same things over and over and expecting different results." It is the record keeping, the evaluation, the retaining of valuable information, and the feedback which elevates the task or goal to the status of a learning experience.

The process increases your momentum. Without it, you begin to backslide. Your goals are suddenly just out of your reach. That promotion goes to someone else. Soon you find that you don't enjoy your work anymore. You tell yourself that it's just not challenging. The truth is that you are failing to meet the challenge.

Remember the Success Spiral and use it to your advantage.

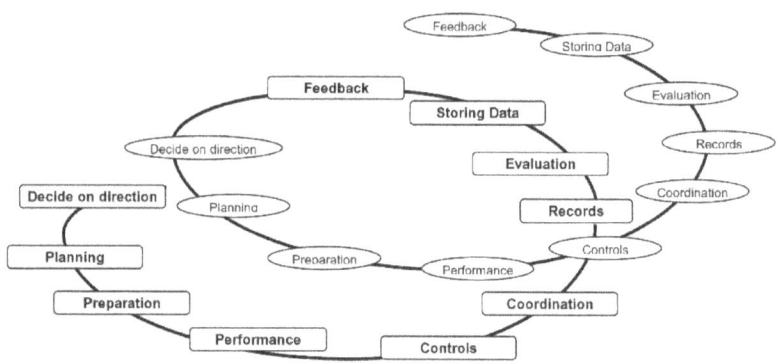

RELATIONSHIPS IN LIFE AND BUSINESS

◐ Friends, Family, and Significant Others

FEAR: A MILESTONE

If you're willing to confront it, fear can be an important milestone in your evolvement. Nothing provokes quite so much thought as fear, and nothing is quite so revealing. However, the things revealed by fear are quite often as cloaked as the fear itself can manage to be, requiring persistence of effort.

The most commonplace fear today is the fear of intimacy. Intimacy is a surfacing of those inner emotions, those inner thoughts, to a conscious level. Many cannot even deal with bringing those feelings to a conscious realization within themselves. The idea of sharing that consciousness with another person is paralyzing.

Most relationships can be likened to a person's first encounter with the high dive. He bounds up the steps, steps out onto the diving board, jumps up and down to build upward momentum, and then ... he freezes, unable to go beyond the point where he must trust himself to his own instincts. Should he fail to complete the dive, he wouldn't flaunt himself to the world as a diver, nor to himself; however, the irony is that what most people consider a relationship today is little more than the show performed on the diving board. Very few venture far enough to take the dive itself.

Why is there such a conspiracy of consciousness to delude us into believing that if we truly open ourselves up to another person, we will only be disappointed? Our fear of intimacy is at the base of this delusion. Fear tends to rationalize attitudes to make them an acceptable mode of behavior. According to Webster, when we rationalize, we are "justifying unconscious behavior". Thus, we justify our failure to "make the dive" by saying that we would only be disappointed. However, the reality is that we are afraid of our performance not being acceptable to others and of being hurt. In a relationship we are afraid of rejection by someone whose opinions have come to matter to us. What is the ultimate result of this rationalization? A lack in our lives. It prevents us from being open and receptive because we have chosen to be selective in what we reveal not only to others, but to ourselves.

How do we overcome this fear? Our first step is honesty with ourselves. When we find ourselves in a relationship which seems to have all the right ingredients, yet we are constantly "spoiling for a fight," instead of blaming the relationship, we need to ask ourselves a few pertinent questions. WHY am I angry at this person? WHY am I so protective of my time and space? Am I afraid this person is causing me to move closer to "taking the dive" and the only way to stop it is to find fault?

The answers to these questions may be painful. However, the most difficult step is yet to come for we must also be honest with the other person in the relationship. We must allow our thoughts, feelings or doubts, to be expressed by us in a sharing, not accusative way.

At this point you may be desperately trying to declare that you have taken the "dive" before, that it was a disaster, and what do I have to say about that? Very simply? That is wonderful if you did indeed have a truly honest, in-depth relationship with another. No one can guarantee us that the person we have chosen is "right," but such a life experience can only serve to teach if we are willing to confront our fears. We must learn to trust in our abilities, not our fear. It is time we cease jumping up and down in place and dive into life, confronting our fears with honesty. There's no way to lose unless we never take a chance.

Who Is The Real Problem In Your Relationships?

Did you know that there are always 4 people in a relationship, not just the usual 2? Knowing this can help you understand a lot about relationships. It helps explain:

- why you have those brief, frustrating, and dead-end relationships
- how a great relationship can, without apparent cause, suddenly turn into such a downer
- why it can be so difficult to talk with someone even though they seemed nice
- why it can be so difficult to have a meaningful conversation with your significant other
- why asking someone for a date requires so much courage.

For those of you who are married, you're probably thinking the other two people in your relationship are your in-laws. Well, they may be trying to insert themselves into the relationship, but that would mean there would be 8 people fighting for their place! So, let's just concentrate on a relationship between you and one other person.

Carl Jung said that getting a better grip on understanding the difficulties between men and women begins by accepting that we are androgynous. Androgyny is a Greek term made up of two words: *andros* and *gynos*. Andros means "male" and gynos means "female." So, if you are androgynous, then whether you are physically male or female, you each contain an *invisible opposite*. This is normally expressed in terms of physicality. In other words, a man while expressing physically as a man has an invisible female or "feeling nature." A woman while expressing physically as a woman has an invisible male or "thinking nature." However, the truth is that your physicality is not necessarily the determinant of your invisible opposite. If your dominant nature is masculine or the "thinking nature," your invisible opposite is the feminine or "feeling nature," and if your dominant nature is feminine, then your invisible opposite is the masculine or "thinking nature."

So, in *any* relationship, there are actually four people involved. Two visible and two invisible. Many of your relationship problems come from the fact that you are not aware that you have an internal, invisible partner who is nonetheless REAL! Most important, your invisible partner expects to be nurtured just like you do.

When you hear people talk about the need to get in touch with your feminine or embrace your intellect, they are responding to a truth. This truth is based on the importance of the relationship between *your dominant nature and your inner opposite.*

Projecting Your Invisible Partner Outward

Why is getting in touch with your inner opposite — your invisible partner — so important? Because it doesn't matter what kind of relationship you are in — marriage, friend, dating, co-worker, they are all influenced by the quality of the relationship you have with your invisible partner.

How does this work? If you are unaware of the attitudes you have toward your inner opposite (your feminine or masculine natures) or refuse to embrace your invisible partner, these attitudes are projected into the relationships you have in the world. In other words, you see these attitudes as coming from **out there** rather than from inside your mental world.

These projections are strong psychic energy, and they can be of a *positive or a negative nature*. They exhibit such powerful energy that you will swear that the object of your affection or the object of your disgust *is out there* and you know his or her name!

How Your Projections Can Manifest

Of course, the relationship you have with your inner opposite ranges in intensity. For clarity, let's consider *<u>extreme</u>* examples:

- If your dominant nature is masculine, and you have a strongly negative relationship with your inner opposite, your projection will cause you to see a woman or a feminine personality in any relationship as a witch. If your projection is strongly positive, that person will seem to be a goddess or an angel, able to do no wrong.

- If your dominant nature is feminine, and you have a strongly negative relationship with your inner opposite, you will see a man or a masculine personality in any relationship as a demon. If your projection is strongly positive, you will see this person as a knight in shining armor, your savior.

In intimate relationships, this ability to *project your relationship with your invisible partner outward* explains why people can fall head over heels at first sight. Falling in love like this is almost always caused by a person projecting a *positive opposite* onto some other person. Our divorce rate is close to 50%. I believe this happens because rather than two real people getting married, two projections get married. When the façade caused by the projection falls away the marriage ends.

Romeo and Juliet are probably a good example of this type of projection. They each projected the highest view of a positive invisible partner onto each other. No human can, for very long, live up to the standard set by such a powerful psychic projection. Sooner or later, the illusion fails, and they fall out of love as dramatically and quickly as they fell into love because these kinds of relationships are not grounded in reality. If the story of Romeo and Juliet had not ended in tragedy, it's unlikely that their relationship would have survived the real world.

The Purpose Of Your Relationships

Once you step into this planet, the relationship with your invisible partner exists in varying degrees of antagonism. Interestingly, people begin life being **totally unaware** that their inner opposite exists and that their primary responsibility is to develop a loving relationship with it.

Let me recount an ancient myth that illustrates the concept of invisible partners. According to the story, there was a time when beings were shaped like spheres. These spherical beings had four arms, four legs and two heads facing in opposite directions. These beings developed tremendous power and made the gods envy and fear them. So the gods cut the spheres in half and scattered them around the planet to divide their power. It is said that when two of these halves find each other, they are joined in a bond of love and harmony.

Most of the time people think this is referring to finding a "soul mate." What the myth is really illustrating is the power you have when you become "at one" with your invisible partner. When this happens, your thoughts (the masculine) and your feelings (the feminine) are in harmony. This harmony enables you to be the fully functioning, creative being you were meant to be.

Fall in Love with Yourself!

This is the planet of lesson. Learning to be in harmony with the sum total of who you are is called being in love with yourself. Love is the glue of the universe. It is the harmonizing magnetic force that draws like things together. *You attract what you are, not what you want.* The more harmony and love you have within yourself, the more you attract its likeness in the world of your relationships.

So, if you're having trouble in a relationship, consider how you feel about your invisible partner.

- Could you be projecting your own insecurities about your feminine or masculine nature onto others?
- If you have trouble talking with one sex or the other, is it possible you're avoiding dealing with your inner opposite?

- If you're sitting across the breakfast table from someone and you feel a subtle dread and an emptiness, could it be mirroring the relationship you have with your invisible partner?
- If you're timid about asking for a date or fearful of accepting one, maybe you're just afraid to get involved with either your feelings or your thoughts.

No one ever said relationships are easy, but it helps to know that there are FOUR people contributing to the quality of a relationship – not just two!

YOU KNOW HOW YOU ARE…

Do your family members tend to pre-judge your reactions to situations? Do they say "Well, you know how you are!" to justify their actions? Do they assume that you're going to handle things the way you did when you were a teenager?

Does it drive you crazy? I know it did me. There was a time when I let it ignite anger within me. Now I tend to ignore it.

But why does it hack you off so much? It's because family members are inclined to hold you in that emotional and psychological place in which you existed when everyone was still living together. In other words, they take the path of least resistance by choosing to see the YOU that is familiar to them. This means that they don't even try to get to know the "real you" – the you that has been growing and changing since you left home.

This is one of the reasons why holidays can be so stressful with family. There is such disparity between the person you were and the person you have become or are striving to become. Your family's efforts to interact with the person with whom they're familiar creates a psychological whiplash effect for you. It isn't long-lasting, but it is extremely painful for the short-term.

What's the solution? Be aware of why your family members do what they do. Don't rise to the occasion by letting your frustrations get the best of you. Be who you are or are striving to become. Eventually, your family will come around. If you fight them, it only increases their determination that they are right about you!

3 WAYS TO SURVIVE GOING HOME FOR THE HOLIDAYS

For many years, I wasn't ready to admit that a visit home for the holidays traumatized me so badly that even after returning home, I was in a dark mood for days and sometimes weeks. I often justified my state of mind by blaming it on the long drive home or the pressure of catching up at work. Then I heard something from Ed Rabel, a teacher of mine, that opened my eyes to the higher purpose intended by the family dynamic. He said, "*Every thing, experience, and circumstance that passes from the realm of possibility into your world of experience has a deeper meaning and purpose. If you don't see this, you're not looking deeply enough.*"

To me, this meant that my experiences at home had a deeper purpose in life than just providing so much useless, unnecessary suffering. But, like the statement says, sometimes this purpose is not all that apparent unless a person looks *past the obvious to find the underlying meaning*. So what I want to do is share with you three ways I learned to not be victimized by visits home for a holiday.

1. **Before You Go Home, Change Your Attitude Toward Your Idea of Family.**

    Rather than seeing your visit as an emotional tug of war, see it as a learning experience. To do this, it helps you to know that you chose your family before you came into this world. The choice you made for parents and siblings was not necessarily so you would have loving, harmonious relationships. Instead, the selection was determined by how you could improve psychologically and spiritually because of what you would be able to learn from your interactions with them. ***So, the individuals in your family who punch your buttons are your teachers.***

    Why is this true? It's because your relationship with them makes you aware of parts of your nature that need to be healed. As a result, they provide you with the opportunity to grow psychologically and spiritually. So, the experience of family, like every experience, "has a deeper meaning and purpose."

To access this meaning, you must look beyond the actions of your family and examine *your reactions* to them. What feelings are awakened by their words or deeds? These are the things that are important. You cannot change your family, but you can use them to change yourself!

2. **To Survive Going Home for the Holidays, You Must Let Go of the Idea that You Have to Like and Please Your Family.**

The individuals in your family are just people, and like anyone else in your social world, you either like them or you don't. You get along with them, or you don't. The truth is that you can never fully live up to their expectations anyhow! Often their approval is like a moving target because it is motivated by their mood of the moment.

So, don't pretend to agree with things you don't agree with just for the sake of keeping the peace. Don't say things that are inconsistent with what you believe. When you do, it is not *just* an energy drain. The emotional tug of war gives you a bad feeling that can stay with you even after you return home.

You might ask the question, "But aren't you supposed to love your family?" Well, yes! You must love them, but you *don't have to like them*. To love someone means you wish them all the good they can accept for themselves. To like someone, on the other hand, means there is a subjective harmony between you.

3. **Taking Charge of Your Feelings is the Third Way To Survive Visits Home For The Holidays.**

Be aware that your involvement with family members is driven by a conditioned reaction. It is not a conscious choice unless you choose to make it one. It's common knowledge that the interaction within the family, especially in the early years, is a powerful force that tends to crystallize a person's place in the family structure.

Targeting Your Potential

Isn't one of the problems with going home for the holidays that your family wants to treat you like you are still a mixed-up teenager, despite the fact that you are perhaps now very successful in life? Also, they may treat your goals like wishful thinking on your part just because you didn't have it together very well when you lived at home. They can't accept that you have changed at all!

Once you acknowledge this crystallized view as a possibility, you have the opportunity to observe what triggers your emotional reactions. When you do, you can make an intellectual and emotional decision to change your response.

So before you go home, bring to mind what you normally say and feel when in the family environment. In other words, **be aware of how your conditioning causes you to adapt your behavior to match what is expected of you by the family.** You must stand *behind* your conditioning so that you can see how it is a put-up job of *your own creation*. Then in your imagination, rehearse what you could say and do to consciously change these encounters. This is the beginning of your own personal declaration of independence, *a brand new version of you.*

Going home for the holidays is never what you envision—at least for most of us. So, why not plan your holidays this year as a *working* holiday? Plan to work on yourself! Be the person you want to be. Don't let the emotional triggers set you off. Don't let your ego get into war with their egos. Use the time to look at the experience as it's happening. Then look deeply within yourself to see where you can change the cycle of your conditioning.

Don't despair if things don't go that well the first time you try this. It may take several holidays for the overall experience to level out. After all, your family will continue to try to nudge you into the position they believe you should hold. Your job is to work on yourself enough that you not only don't slip into that position, you don't even notice the nudging.

BUILDING STRONG RELATIONSHIPS

Relationships That Do Not Require Intimacy

We have many different kinds of relationships throughout our lives – even throughout the day. The bases for these relationships are different. For example, your relationship with the people at work or with a shopkeeper is based, at least initially, on economic exchange. Some are based on group memberships, such as church or school. Other relationships exist because of mutual friends or because you routinely encounter them at the store or at child care, for example. We eat out a lot, and we regularly develop relationships with the waiters and waitresses. Even the conversational give-and-take with fellow customers in a store can feel rewarding. I am from the South, and in the South people tend to be open and friendly with complete strangers. I was used to that and did not realize until we moved away how important a role those relationships played in my life.

However, the one thing all these types of relationships have in common is that they *do not require intimacy*. So it is important to understand that viable relationships do exist without the need for intimacy.

Relationships That Do Require Intimacy

However, relationships that are forged because of a common goal do require intimacy. What would those be? Of course, partner/spouse relationships would be one, but it also includes relationships such as those you forge in church when you are committed to the growth of the organism called church. It includes family relationships, close friendships. Football players form intimate relationships because they have a strong, singular goal — winning. In the workplace, power team members often form closer relationships with each other because of the experience of being part of the focused effort of the team.

Dimensions Of Intimacy

Intimacy involves closeness, and it has three dimensions: physical, emotional, and intellectual.

- **Physical** intimacy is quite common for most people when they are growing up if their family is not too dysfunctional to be affectionate. However, once we grow into adults, we tend to back off from people. Touching is not always a part of accepted social interaction. Fortunately, in my spiritual group, we try to bridge that chasm by engaging in hugs. In a sexual relationship, of course, physical intimacy is very important. However, physical intimacy of any kind, whether it's sexual, a hug, a hand on the shoulder, or just shaking hands, is important in a relationship because it creates a bond, a connection.

- The **emotional** dimension of intimacy involves the sharing of *feelings*. There are guidelines, of course, for sharing your feelings. The sexual freedom exercised today often diminishes this emotional bond that is part of an intimate relationship. The *one-night stands* people talk about actually fall into the casual type of relationships you have with the bus driver or the beautician who does your hair. Why? Because there is no commitment to the relationship.

- The **intellectual** dimension of intimacy naturally involves the sharing of *ideas* or thoughts. Discussions between two people in a constructive environment that involve a give and take about ideas can be very powerful. This is why it is not uncommon to find two people working on the same project who escalate into a sexual relationship. Their intimacy began in the dimension of the intellect and moved into an intense emotional and then physical intimacy.

Of course, the quality of a relationship is not determined by whether or not it expresses in all three dimensions. Every relationship has three dimensions of intimacy; it is the degree of *mutual* commitment to those elements that determines the quality of the relationship. In other words, is there give and take to the satisfaction of **both** parties?

The Need for Distance

While intimacy is an important element in relationships, so is distance. Everyone needs their space, even with partners or spouses or family or close friends. With less intimate relationships, the need for distance is often literal. In the United States, people tend to keep a distance of at least 3 feet when talking to each other. Invading that space will often make others uncomfortable, especially if you are not that familiar to them.

However, in closer relationships, the need for distance usually means time to ourselves and/or a place that is private. I know that some of you have a study or a den that you call your own, or you set aside a certain time of day that you are not to be disturbed by anyone, or maybe you go for walks alone. Perhaps you spend hours browsing in the bookstore. Whatever the activity, it is designed to give you time to be with yourself. It is a time to reflect, to assess your day, to consider something that is bothering you, or just to re-center yourself.

Creating time for yourself in a relationship is extremely important. Unless you nurture yourself, you will have nothing to give to the other person. And, a relationship is nothing unless there is **give and take.**

What Determines The People To Whom We Are Attracted?

1. **Similarities** would seem to be the most obvious. How often have you desired to have people of like-mind in your life? When you meet someone, don't you usually try to find some common ground? Something you can both talk about? Of course you do! It is a natural tendency.

It is not necessary to be *exactly* like someone else to get along. That might actually be pretty boring! You just need to have enough in common to create a foundation from which the relationship can grow. These similarities can be attitudes, talents, or experiences. It doesn't matter just as long as you find some common ground.

2. The second point of attraction is **differences**. This may sound like it is contradicting the first point about similarities, but it isn't. If the differences between you are complementary, they will strengthen a relationship. A popular cliché is "opposites attract." This is only true if the characteristics of one satisfies the needs of the other.

For example, if a man is an addictive personality – perhaps alcohol or rage, then the person who best complements him is an enabler. A person whose need to make another's life work needs someone who requires either an accomplice or a victim in order to justify or support his addiction. Now this is not a very positive example of a relationship, but in reality, it is a relationship that works. Just because a relationship does not contribute to spiritual and emotional well-being does not mean that it is not satisfying the needs of those involved.

3. Next – we like **people who like us**! Why not? That seems like a pretty good head start on a relationship to me. Of course, it is important to be aware that it is often our false personality— our ego — that is responding to adulation from someone else. So it is important not to build a relationship solely on vanity. As time passes, take the time to ask yourself if the relationship is one-sided. Are you allowing the other person to believe the relationship is more intimate than it is simply because it is feeding your ego?

4. The next factor sounds rather cold at first. It is based on what is called the **exchange theory**. We can easily see this in less intimate relationships. For example, a business partnership between two people is often based on the fact that what each has to offer the other

is worth any discomfort that arises from being in close proximity. Of course, this also applies to intimate relationships. How many of you have certain things you could list that your partner does that drives you up the wall? Everyone does. However, we tolerate their quirks because of the positive benefits we receive from their friendship.

5. **Competence** is the fifth attracting element. However, we temper that by requiring they have some flaws. So you can quit trying to be perfect. People like you better when you're not!

Like everything else in life, there are exceptions. People at the opposite ends of the bell curve of self-esteem do find so called "perfect people" attractive. People with extremely high self-esteem seek perfection because they often feel it is the ultimate goal. Those with extremely low self-esteem seek those who appear to be perfect because it allows them to feel justified in their low self-esteem.

6. **Disclosure** plays an important role in attraction, but it is important that it is done appropriately. Disclosure can reveal similarities between you. If you are obviously struggling with some situation, such as a divorce, and someone says privately to you: "I went through a divorce recently, too, and it was emotionally devastating," you are probably going to bond with them immediately. Misery does love company! If, however, they say, "I just got a divorce, and it went off without a hitch", well ... your first reaction might be to strangle them!

Disclosure of personal information can also indicate that the other person respects and trusts you. If, however, they share *way more* than you are willing to share, you may find yourself feeling uncomfortable. So it is important that the amount and content of the disclosure is appropriate.

7. **Proximity** plays an important role in attraction. Office romances and close friendships that develop with co-workers attest to that. It is

not just convenience that makes proximity a factor. It is because you are able to gradually gather information about a person and benefit from a relationship with them when you interact with them more frequently.

Developmental Stages in Intimate Relationships

The rise and fall of *intimate* relationships outside the family has been outlined in a model developed by Mark Knapp. According to Knapp there are two processes that occur in these relationships: *coming together* and *coming apart*. That seems pretty obvious even to the casual observer. Each of these processes, however, has five developmental stages.

The first process — coming together — has the following stages: *Initiating, Experimenting, Intensifying, Integrating, and Bonding.*

In the first stage of coming together, **Initiating**, you indicate that you are interested in making contact. A simple "Hello. How are you?" or a handshake or any acknowledgement that you are willing to interact initiates the relationship. You have made the first move.

In the second stage, **Experimenting**, you try to get more information to see if you are interested in pursuing the relationship. Small talk is prevalent in this stage. Remember what we said about searching for common ground when we talked about the elements of attraction? Well, in this stage, you are asking yourself, "Is this worth investing my energy?" I know that sounds rather self-absorbed, but it is a natural instinct to conserve energy for those things which enhance one's experiences in life. Now, remember, we're not talking about casual relationships. We're talking about close, intimate relationships. In the experimenting stage, the small talk shifts from questions to personal disclosure. Consequently, attraction increases.

In the third stage, **Intensifying**, emotional communication characterizes the relationship. It can be direct and indirect. Indirect communication is exchanged through acting in ways that show love and concern for the other person and their feelings. Direct communication involves discussing the nature of your feelings about the relationship. You may express feelings of commitment. Often during the third stage of the relationship, the level of commitment is tested. There are many ways of doing this – creating challenges that require proof of commitment, hinting to get expressions of commitment [such as waiting to hear an "I love you, too" from the other person], scouting out others to find out if they've heard anything you should know, and the old stand-by: trying to make your partner jealous.

In the fourth stage, **Integrating**, the relationship strengthens, and the antics in the third stage cease. You are now seen as a unit, a couple, by others. You start taking on the commitments of your partner, such as spending the holidays with their family. You start to have common property. You may even develop your own method of communication.

Let me share a personal story about unique communication. I have always had a good memory, but not for jokes. My husband was always telling me jokes, but I could never remember the joke itself later. If he mentioned the punch line of the joke, however, I would always laugh with as much joy as I had the first time. I remembered that it was funny; I just couldn't remember why, but once I started to laugh, there was no stopping it. We would both be laughing hysterically in a few minutes. So it finally developed to the stage where he could say punch lines like "It must be the salt water," and I would laugh so hard tears would roll. We have enjoyed this private communication immensely over the years, but anyone else would swear we were nuts!

The second process in the rise and fall of *intimate* relationships outside the family — *coming apart* — occurs in these five stages: *Differentiating, Circumscribing, Stagnating, Avoiding, and Terminating*.

1. In the first stage of *coming apart*, we find two people who have bonded, which was the last stage in the *coming together* process. Now they feel a need to re-establish their personal identities. They sense a need for privacy instead of the all-encompassing closeness experienced previously. **Differentiation** does not have to be a bad thing. It is important for individuals in any kind of relationship to be independent, and the relationship can continue to work well as long as there is a commitment to the relationship.

2. The second stage is **Circumscribing**. This is the first stage that truly has to do with the decline of a relationship. The earlier stage of differentiation can go either way depending on the commitment level. If the relationship is moving toward decline, this stage will involve less commitment and lack of interest. In practical terms, an unwillingness to discuss issues, the silent treatment, and perhaps a great deal of fantasizing characterize this stage.

3. The third stage is **Stagnating**. I think the mental image of what happens in this stage is pretty obvious. It's called "going through the motions." We've seen it in people at work who can no longer stand their jobs, and between friends and lovers who no longer have the same interests.

4. The fourth stage is **Avoiding**. People start making excuses to keep from dealing with the intimacy of being together for any reason.

It is important to note here that the one thing that can turn a relationship around during this time of *coming apart* is COMMUNICATION. Holding your thoughts and feelings inside rather than constructively discussing them only serves to create a cancer that feeds on itself.

5. The fifth stage is **Terminating**, which is just what it sounds like. Terminations can be amicable or nasty. The parties can remain

friendly, but without the previous closeness. It depends a great deal on the quality of communication during this stage.

The movement between the stages of a relationship is not always linear. There are always tugs that occur because of the nature of the stages. For example, the need for independence can create a circumstance that alternates between being closely bonded and maintaining autonomy. Just keep in mind that a relationship will be always changing — either coming together or coming apart, getting deeper or becoming more superficial.

Targeting Your Potential

WHAT HAPPENS WHEN YOU MOURN?

Eventually all relationships come to an end. I went to the funeral of a family member, and the only feeling I had was guilt. I felt guilty because I felt nothing. For years this bothered me. How could I be such a stone — so cold and unfeeling? I began to wonder why some people were overwhelmed by a person's death and others seemed unaffected. I found the answer, not in the Bible or any psychological study, but in the world of science.

Scientist say that a plant absorbs from the earth and the sun the necessary energy, moisture, and other elements that it needs to grow into a mature plant. When the plant dies, all of what it took from its surroundings is returned.

In the same way, all of the emotional energy you invest in a relationship is released when for some reason the connection between you is broken.

Just as there are different levels of quality and strength in plants, there are different levels of strength in the relationships between people. This strength is determined by how much emotional energy is invested in the relationship.

In other words, when we invest very little feeling into a relationship, the connection has little strength. When a lot of emotional energy is invested in a relationship, a strong bond is created.

When a strong connection between individuals is broken, the energy that was invested in the relationship is released ***through the survivor***. As this passes through him or her, it expresses as the pain we call ***mourning*** or ***grieving***.

In my mind, this accounts for the differences in people's reactions when they lose someone, whether it's from death or separation. The *more* emotional energy – whether positive or negative – invested in a relationship, the more pain we experience. The less emotional energy invested, the less affected we are.

Don't jump to conclusions about mourning, however. It is not about the outer reactions that the rest of us see. Mourning is an internal experience. Whether a person appears to grieve or not has nothing to do with the inner pain they may be feeling. We see this on television all the time when people judge the parent of a missing child as guilty because they are not publicly falling apart. My late sister and I were polar opposites. All her feelings jumped right out there for all to see; whereas, I keep mine under control until I am in my private space.

Regardless of how you deal with your pain, just knowing that mourning is simply the return of your invested energy back into the Universe can help you pass through the grieving process without inflicting psychological damage on yourself.

◐ Co-workers/Associates

CREATING A SENSE OF FAMILY IN THE WORKPLACE

The word *family*, originally from the Latin, meant "servant" and was used to refer to all the domestic servants of a household. Once its usage entered English, *family* gradually broadened to include the whole household and eventually narrowed down to "a group of related people."

So what does *family* have to do with the workplace? It has a great deal actually. Those working for the same company come to work on average 5 days out of 7 and spend approximately 8 hours of those days with each other. Discounting the average time you are asleep each week, you spend 36% of your waking time together! The time involved and the common focus of your time while you are in the workplace certainly places you in the category of a "group of related people."

Sociologically, a functional family serves several functions:

a) assists in the acquisition and internalization of beliefs and attitudes,
b) provides a general sense of well-being, companionship, ego worth, security, and affection,
c) provides meaningful social experiences.

Loyalty to *family* is a very strong emotion. For those of you who did not have a healthy biological family environment, the workplace often takes the place of that familiarity you seek.

Consequently, business owners and employees need to address the workplace from a perspective *other than economic*. Most of the difficulties in the workplace can be attributed to the same conflicts that are endemic to dysfunctional relationships. These conflicts are caused by the lack of several things: **creative living, communication, respect, support, and trust.**

To reduce dysfunction in the workplace, you must learn how to develop the attitudes or qualities which serve to resolve or avoid conflict. If you look up *effective management* in any textbook, you will likely see the results of such management described this way: 1) *achieving the best possible results* 2) *without wasting money, time, or energy.* Unfortunately, the second point is often the entire focus of managers. They consider the best route to effective management as streamlining or eliminating any procedures that are believed not to be cost or time effective. This is an economic decision and completely disregards the actions needed to get the *best* results for all concerned.

In the chapter on The Success Spiral, we talked about some of these ideas in terms of your individual success. Now we are looking at the interactions in the workplace between management and staff that can build functional relationships that produce success for all involved.

Attitude #1: Creative Living

There is merit in the old standard approach to management, but if you want to reach new levels of production, you have to be willing to be **creative**. You must allow your mind to be continually seeking, searching, wondering, and experimenting with the concepts involved in your operations. It is not necessary to always approach a project with linear thinking or to always do it the "way it's always been done."

Involving others in the process through brainstorming is a viable concept. Most of us have experienced brainstorming sessions; however, in business, they usually only involve those at one's own level in the hierarchy. It can be just as effective, if not more so, to involve many of those who will be doing most of the work.

At first, brainstorming between management and staff may be difficult because it is a new relationship. Like all new relationships there is a certain awkwardness initially. Once everyone gets used to the idea that management actually cares what the staff thinks, it will be amazing to hear the ideas which emerge.

These sessions should address all aspects of the project which involve the cooperation of the staff or affect them in any way. All suggestions should be considered seriously with the pros and cons discussed. Many attitude problems can be resolved in this way because the process may reveal things of which some of the people involved are not aware. Consequently, you become able to understand why certain things are done the way they are, which can reduce conflict in the day-to-day arena.

Attitude #2: Communication

Once you have creatively determined what you want your result to be and what creative methods you intend to use to accomplish it, the next step is **communication**. Despite the fact that many or even all of the staff were involved in the initial planning, a written plan should be presented, noting that it is a result of **department planning**!

It should reiterate:

- *what* you decided to do,
- *when* you need it done,
- *where* the various responsibilities lie, and
- most important, *why* you are doing this project or doing it in this way if different from past efforts. This reduces misunderstandings and gives the staff a vested interest in its success.

You've been hearing about positive thinking for years. Well, the positive *energy* that results from this approach is real. If those working with you are investing positive energy into what you are doing, it is destined to succeed because it takes on a life of its own, evolving and changing in a productive way. Positive energy sparks creativity, and because every employee has a special perspective, you'll discover that those directly involved are able to fine-tune the project in a way that managers cannot.

Attitude #3: Performance

The next stage involves **performance** of the planned steps. Performance should again be an interactive process because it opens the door for staff to present new and creative ideas to management along the way. Management is not a closed system. Without input from those hired for their special skills, management's effectiveness is minimized.

Attitude #4: Responsibilities

When the various **responsibilities** of the project are allocated, care should be taken to make sure that the staff understands the level of responsibility involved in each instance. With *explicit* responsibility, the guidelines should be written out clearly for the staff member. If the responsibility is *implied* within the project guidelines, this authority should still be verbally communicated to the staff member.

Implicit responsibility means that management is granting the staff member the right to make decisions in their job area if situations arise out of the ordinary. This means their skills *and* their experience are being affirmed. If an employee has mastered the job, implicit responsibility is a teaching tool. It is also a sign of respect and support from the employer.

Attitude #5: Serve and Trust

Many employees are lost to other companies due to fear by management. You fear their decisions. Sometimes you fear their abilities because you fear losing your own position to them. The only way to be a successful manager is to **serve and trust**.

Targeting Your Potential

As *managers*, you must serve the company for which you work, but you must also serve those you manage and trust their skills (and your decision to hire them). You have a responsibility to draw from them their very best, *not* just for the sake of the company, but for their sake.

As *employees*, you must serve the company as well and trust that those in management positions have your best interests at heart. If you treat each other as family with all the respect and support that implies, everyone prospers! It's a win-win situation.

So, reach out into your work environment and take advantage of this pool of energy, which is never-ending if it is tapped for the benefit of everyone involved—the *family!*

▷ Networking

ARE YOU A NETWORKER, A GATHERER, OR A COLLECTOR?

Networkers, from an entrepreneurial perspective, are people who reach out to other professionals with whom they believe they can establish alliances built on the idea of *mutual support*. These individuals should have common interests and objectives. This alliance is built on the understanding that there is give-and-take. There is a flow between you.

Gatherers are people who inhale business cards like an addict inhales cocaine. They are gathering names, addresses, and emails without concern for the flow between themselves and others. They are searching for *targets for their products*. If you meet one of these people at an event, you rarely get to share anything about your own entrepreneurial adventure. You exchange cards and listen quietly as they expound upon the virtues of their product.

Collectors. Collectors are the scariest of all. These are the ones who collect people, not business cards. They search for people who can enhance what they do with no concern for the other's needs. The objects [people] in their collection are viewed as **utilitarian**. *Which ones can I use to make this project work for me?* There are no thoughts of reciprocity. If the "object" happens to benefit, the Collector considers it a bonus for himself because it strengthens his hold on this prize object. The Collector lists his contacts the same way the rest of us list our office equipment.

So, which are you?

Gatherers

We have all been gatherers at times. There is nothing wrong with occasionally sending out email notices/announcements to people you have met through networking meetings. It is expected at a certain level. However, a gatherer is his own worst enemy. If you continuously send daily or weekly or even twice a month sales pitches to people—*not customers*—with whom your only connection is a business card, your email correspondence will hit the trash the moment they see your name. You join the ranks of the spammers who send all those emails about pharmaceuticals!

A gatherer can remedy the dead-end quality of his situation by taking the time to *actually network* with some of his contacts who fall into categories that harmonize with his own business.

Make a phone call. Set up a coffee date. Let them know you are interested in investigating the possibility of a *mutually supportive* relationship with them. Emphasize that it is not a sales pitch! If you aren't able to determine some way to help each other at this point, at least you established a personal contact. That person has a better sense of you and you of them. These types of connections will provide a stronger return on your investment down the road than most advertising.

Collectors

What about a collector? This one is much more difficult. To create a clearer picture, let's compare the *motives* of the Gatherer and the Collector.

The motive of a gatherer usually stems from an uneducated perspective that more is better. Assault as many people as possible with your product, and the law of averages is in your favor. Of course, this is not really true. Even if there is a short surge of success, it falters shortly unless your product is so outstanding that word of mouth takes over. Unfortunately, this rarely happens because before the gatherer is able to close the sale with a deluge of sales pitches, he has already been automatically delegated to the trash bin!

The collector, on the other hand, is motivated purely from *self-aggrandizement*. His contacts are chosen on the basis of how useful they are for enhancing or exaggerating the collector's importance, power, or reputation. In other words, he gathers purely for the purpose of exalting himself. Of course, some collectors are aware of their motivation while others actually believe their own hype.

If you know someone who is a collector, walk carefully. You may or may not be at financial risk, but the emotional risk that comes with being objectified, which demeans you and your business or profession, can have debilitating effects for an entrepreneur. This is especially true for budding entrepreneurs.

If you are a collector, it is time for you to consider that life is designed for give-and-take. You can't always take. Eventually, even the pretense you depend on of having "something of value that others want" will start to deteriorate. Flow requires that energy flows in, and then be able to flow out. It is not designed to be "collected."

Networkers

A networker is a person who becomes part of a net — an interwoven or intertwined structure — of contacts who depend on each other for support. You make referrals to others in the network. You offer opportunities to them. You are available for mentoring and seek it as well. You see the others in the network as human beings with their own sacred journey, and you honor that. Within a true network, these actions are reciprocated without question.

A true networker does not *expect* others to give their time freely to his venture. He honors others' talents and abilities. So, unless it is a joint venture where both expect to benefit financially, payment for services is the chosen path, again without question.

So, who are you and who would you rather be? A Gatherer, a Collector, or a Networker?

Targeting Your Potential

A HIGHER VIEW OF NETWORKING

Integration

All actions in life are responses to needs. Those needs may be physical or psychological/spiritual. As a teacher, author, and counselor, my perspective is based on the belief that we are "spiritual beings having a human experience." So, naturally, when I observe an event in the world, I look toward the psychological/spiritual to see the threads that are influencing the intention behind the event.

When I look at the world in this way, I see a lattice of threads that connect us all in many different ways. As I watch someone struggling to grow their business, I see the newly-formed threads their business efforts are weaving; however, I also see the catalytic threads that exist on a grander scale and that drew them in this particular direction on a wondrous journey of creation.

Networking groups should desire to provide networking support for people in their burgeoning efforts to establish places for themselves, and this should echo in every nuance of the experience you have at one of these gatherings. The greater the intensity of a networking group toward focusing on the success of this networking concept, the more prosperous the group will be — a goal that is common to us all.

This focused and inclusive approach to networking creates threads that connect their efforts to a strong spiritual movement in the world — a move to reach beyond the obstacles we place between us by instead focusing on our similarities. In other words, seeking to INTEGRATE, to work as a whole by bringing everyone together in harmony. I believe this movement exists outside the conscious awareness of most, but people are responding to it nonetheless. The power of any networking group lies in providing a "safe place" for people to relate without the barriers we usually allow to exist between us.

Connection

As we've mentioned before, when two or more persons get together with common interests or goals, often you can "feel" the energy, even to the point of experiencing a "high" psychologically speaking. As two objects begin interaction, what was once potential energy (energy that was unavailable to you) becomes kinetic energy or energy in motion.

When people use this energy to CONNECT, they are rewarded with feelings of elation, joy, accomplishment, and of being in the flow of life. This is the energy you should feel at any networking group that is focused on the success of everyone there. If your group comes together with this kind of networking in mind, the Universe will respond with continual bursts of energy that energize you long after you've all gone home for the evening. What a blessing!

Momentum

Do not be surprised by the tremendous MOMENTUM gained by a networking group with this mindset. The sheer force of all the energy being released at these types of gatherings will propel them forward. They have the potential of creating authentic communities which not only serve the individual, but nurture harmony on a much grander scale.

Bottom Line

Setting aside our differences [**Integration**] so that we can access the abundance of kinetic energy available to us when we come together in support of one another [**Connection**] will undeniably result in a tremendous rush toward achievement for all involved [**Momentum**].

Targeting Your Potential

SET PRIORITIES TO NETWORK EFFECTIVELY

Networking seems to be the magic word today, but it is important that you determine the *value* of your networking. Otherwise, you are just occupying yourself with "busy work" and taking away valuable energy from the heart of your business.

In every field where it appears there is money to be made, there are those who are jumping to the head of the line to be the ones to take your money with promises of great returns. Unfortunately, many networking group organizers are in it for the wrong reasons and, therefore, cannot offer you the benefits they promise.

- Yes, it is true that **having a venue for connecting with others is important**; however, if those connections are all being made with people who are also at the budding stage of their entrepreneurial efforts, they are less interested in your business and more focused on *your* interest in *their* product as we mentioned in the last chapter. The reason for this, of course, is that they are desperate to establish a viable income. Consequently, few sales are made by anybody and few financially beneficial connections follow.

  One of the first things you learn in trying to market your business is to make it larger-than-life. In other words, you don't start out by saying – *I've been in business for eight months, but I still don't have a viable income. I believe my product is good, but I haven't been able to convince enough other people of it to make a living yet.* So most people give their spiel with the intent of making you believe that they are already so successful they can hardly stand it!

  After getting to know a lot of the people in the networking groups on a personal level, I realized that less than 5% of them are actually making a stand-alone income from their businesses. Most are working other jobs to support themselves, or their spouse is supporting the family, or they are hanging on by a thread. As a result, the exchanges that happen with most fellow networkers is in the form of bartering. This can be good, but ultimately, it does not pay your bills.

- **Time is one of your most important assets as an entrepreneur.** Networking can eat up this asset and leave you with no time for taking care of your business. In many groups you are constantly being called upon to prepare presentations or participate in one event or another. Plus, in many of these groups, the demand for referrals is so great that just coming up with names for others can become a full time job. Many entrepreneurs are handicapped by this because they work out of their homes and don't have endless face-to-face access to customers or colleagues as a referral pool.

So, am I saying that networking has no value? No, of course not! Networking is an important part of growing your business. However, you have to establish priorities for your energies if networking is to be of benefit.

- **The first place you have to invest your energy is in the heart of your business.** People are always eager to use your business to promote their business. Your payment for this is *exposure*. Exposure is a wonderful thing, but not all exposure is worth your time or energy. If you let yourself get caught up in the rush of offers for exposure, you will wake up one morning and discover that your passion for your business has taken a back seat. What good is exposure for your business if you don't have time for your business any more?
- **Understand that the purpose of networking is to benefit your business.** Do not let yourself fall prey to the idea that your business is a cog in the Great Wheel of Networking. The truth is

that your networking efforts are just one cog among all the gears in the *machinery of your business*. You cannot afford to lose this perspective or your business will suffer.

- **Don't believe it!** *"Unless you're networking, you're not working."* It's a great catch phrase for networking group leaders, but unless you have your priorities straight, adopting this attitude can be a death knell for your business. Why? For all the reasons I have just been discussing. You can fall victim to the demands of networking at the expense of developing the foundations for your business.

Oh, I know that there will be people who read this and lament that I just don't understand networking, but I do. I understand that networking can have great value.

1. I understand that it is a necessary element in developing a successful business.
2. I understand that valuable contacts (and friends) can be made through networking.
3. I understand that it can encourage you when you most need encouragement.
4. I *also* understand, however, the sweet allure of being around other entrepreneurial spirits. The camaraderie, however, can make you vulnerable to emotion-based decisions.

That's why it is important to remain balanced with both feet planted in *your own* business. Any decisions you make related to networking groups or fellow networkers have to involve intellectual, emotional, and action perspectives. In other words, you should consider the ramifications for yourself in all these areas. It's just as important not to be an ***enabler*** in business as it is in your personal life.

By all means — NETWORK! — but stay centered. Remember *why* you're networking, and don't let the demands of others use up all your time. Stay focused.

Fitting In: Small Group Dynamics

Learn To Influence Your Interactions In Groups

Groups are inevitable unless you lock yourself in your room. Even then, your flight from groups is only temporary because eventually you will need others for many different reasons.

All of life breaks down into relationships. Any interaction constitutes a relationship. Of course, these relationships may differ by the numbers involved, intensity, and complexity as well as a host of other characteristics. When your relationships involve at least two other people with common goals or problems, or with some bond such as birth, reciprocal abilities, or complementary needs, you are participating in a group dynamic. Because our society functions through the use of groups, it is imperative that you understand how to fit into the group of which you desire to be a part.

If you are an entrepreneur, it is extremely likely that you will find yourself involved in one or more of the networking or referral groups we've been discussing. Many of these groups are membership-based, which means that the group had already formed before you entered the picture. This can be a stressful experience, not unlike changing high schools mid-term when you were a teenager. You could see that friendships and trust were already established among those at the new school. Why would they be interested in you?

To be blunt, the primary interest in you by these networking groups is probably self-serving. They want to promote their business to you with the hope that either you or your contacts will become customers. However, it is up to you to shift their attention away from themselves long enough to take a positive interest in you. How do you influence the interaction you will have with a group?

- First, you have to **perform an assessment**. Ask yourself how different or similar you are to the people in the group. Because some groups are static, this is easier. However, the attendees for some groups vary from meeting to meeting. In that case, you have to assess whether your goals or intentions are different or similar from the group as a whole because you cannot focus on individual personality characteristics.

- Second, **determine the impression you want to make** on the group. Everyone has weaknesses they are trying to overcome. So you certainly don't want them to be an integral part of the image others have of you. In terms of your business, what strength do you need to accentuate? Are there habits or mannerisms that you might need to tone down to fit into this particular group?

- Third, decide **how much of a commitment you're willing to make** to other group members. Do you want to maintain only business relationships? Or are you willing to become friends outside the group? Are you willing to help others without immediate return if you have some needed expertise not directly related to your product or service?

- Fourth, **ask yourself if you are committed to the goals of the group as a whole.** In those groups that are non-membership-based, this is not always as pertinent an issue. However, in most groups, particularly those identified by a specific task, it is totally relevant to the group's success.

- Fifth, ask yourself **if you are prepared to compromise**. Compromise is about working with others to combine the best qualities or elements of different ideas in order to create a workable plan. It is not about conceding to something detrimental to anyone. So, are you dedicated to the principle of win/win? Or do you feel that the only way you can win is if someone else loses?

- Sixth, will you **work toward trusting your fellow members?** Hardly anyone would promise to trust a group of strangers, and I'm not saying you should. What I am saying is that you should commit to allowing that element of your relationships to develop. You have to consciously set aside your paranoia, not your common sense.

If you address the listed items honestly, you will find that your encounters with the group in question will draw you back to these questions over and over in the beginning. You will re-assess as your knowledge about the group increases. You may even discover that your own goals or intentions for participating shift. Sometimes that shift will cause you to leave certain groups. That's okay.

If You Have To Leave A Group, Make The Most Of It!

Sometimes it is not only necessary but beneficial to walk away from some groups in which you've been investing energy. If you do leave, however, it would be prudent for you to examine your thoughts and feelings about your decision.

Consider the 5 W's. These all approach the same answers with different questions. But perhaps one of these questions will alert you to the primary reason you made the decision to leave the group.

1. Is there a WHO causing me to leave the group? If so, write down all the reasons you are allowing this person to control your experience.

2. WHAT specific experience led me to make the decision to leave, if any? Did someone embarrass you or hurt your feelings? Are you not getting referrals? Are you not being allowed the same status in this group as in others?

3. WHEN did I change my mind about the group? This helps you determine if your decision is actually connected to an event—one that you would prefer to forget!

4. WHERE did I expect this group to take me that it failed to do? We often have unconscious and unrealistic expectations about

our involvement with a group, and it leads to our being disgruntled without being able to pinpoint why.

5. WHY is it in my best interests to leave this group? List all the advantages—not the reasons—of your leaving this group.

Understand Your Role in the Group

Unless you are able to analyze your experiences in a group, your experiences will not improve. Of course, there are many groups that you participate in that seem to work wonderfully. That's great! We all have interactions that are pleasing, supportive, and reciprocal. However, it is through the groups that are necessary for upgrading your job/business, your social life, etc. that you encounter the most conflict and yet can benefit from the most if you take the time to understand your role in them.

Different tensions arise during the varying stages of a group. You can see that the tensions that might be present when you first enter a group, such as what motivated you to be there and whether you are able to become part of the existing clique, are different from the tensions that might arise later after you've been assimilated into the group.

Then the tensions might be related to how much time you want to take away from your own business to promote the group or perhaps you're being asked to be a mentor and you really want to be the student. Recognizing these tensions as normal stages of group life keeps you from over-reacting to them.

Because you are now making sense of the environment in each group and your place in it through self-observation, you are better able to:

- communicate effectively
- maintain the delicate balance between relational and task-oriented issues necessary for solid decision-making

- manage the tensions that arise in any group at any stage.

Fitting in is not about giving up who you are. Fitting in is about working on yourself so that you can achieve your full potential. If you're constantly at odds with everyone, how do you expect to benefit from the relationships or receive the rewards that group participation can offer?

Targeting Your Potential

REVIEW QUESTIONS: TARGETING YOUR POTENTIAL

1. What traps a person into thinking small?
2. If you refuse to take action, to commit to your goal, what happens?
3. If you wake up one day and wonder why your work isn't fun anymore, what is a possible solution?
4. What is the critical difference between a self-help program and the Creative Process?
5. Out of the 7 tips listed for finding a quality self-help program, which 3 do you feel are most important to you?
6. What are two ways to rid yourself of attitudes that will sabotage your creative process?
7. What is the most important thing to keep in mind when you are pushing toward an important goal in your life?
8. What are two important things you must do to develop a prosperity state of mind?
9. What determines the energy that your work, whether it is a product or a service, carries with it, encouraging others to pass on their experience with it?
10. If your business is not as much fun as it used to be, what has likely happened?
11. What are the three ways that people generally approach a crisis, and which way applies to you?
12. Review the 9 steps for approaching a crisis.

Targeting Your Potential

13. If a business relationship has one goal-oriented partner and an ego-driven partner, can you explain why it is unlikely that the business will be successful?
14. What do you develop in order to hide your flaws from yourself?
15. If a person is struggling to change their life and refusing to participate in activities and relationships that are spiritually and emotionally damaging, would they fit the definition of a "Me First" person?
16. What are the axioms that a person described in question #15 understands?
17. What is a good question to ask yourself when you are encountering a problem or an opportunity in your life?
18. When you create a goal, why do you have to be able to accept it as being realistic?
19. What are the four characteristics of your venture that you must assess if you want clarity about your goal?
20. What are the eight unique steps involved in the Success Spiral?
21. What is the most commonplace fear today?
22. Why are there four people in any relationship?
23. Why is it so frustrating when your family treats you as if you haven't changed since you were a teenager?
24. What are three ways to survive going home for the holidays?
25. What are the dimensions of intimacy?
26. What are the two processes that occur in relationships?
27. What are the five stages in the first process listed in #26?
28. What are the five stages in the second process listed in #26?
29. What is the process occurring that causes pain when you mourn?

30. What are the five areas that are necessary for functional relationships?
31. Describe a gatherer, a collector, and a networker.
32. What are the three main elements in developing a higher view of networking?
33. Can you explain why these are important?
34. What is one of the most important things you should do to make sure that networking is an asset rather than a liability for your business and how do you do this?
35. When trying to fit into small group dynamics, what are the six items you must consider if you want to influence your interactions with the group?
36. Explain the five W's that you should consider before deciding to leave a group?

Targeting Your Potential

CONCLUSION

Recapping the journey we have taken, we approached two main ideas: developing a fearless attitude and targeting your potential.

To **DEVELOP A FEARLESS ATTITUDE**, you must first *build a foundation*. You must learn to be open and receptive, take charge of your life, and determine how you want to view yourself. Then you must invest energy in your inner growth. It is necessary to understand the connection between your thoughts and feelings and the life you are living. All sorts of issues come up in this process, including the discipline of choices, discerning when blind faith is acceptable and when it is not, recognizing the pull of your soul toward spiritual growth, and learning the relationship between your personality and your essence. Finally, you should familiarize yourself with the spiritual tools available to you.

Once you have a foundation in place, you begin the *healing* process by breaking old patterns, recognizing the power of the subpersonalities within you, learning to express yourself with purpose, and by paying attention to your feelings.

The final stage in developing a fearless attitude deals with *strategies*. Learn how to exploit your weaknesses and how to set goals and give intention. Be willing to step out into the unknown and to redefine your life.

To **TARGET YOUR POTENTIAL**, you should first understand the *creative process*. What are the steps for manifesting your desires, how do you identify programs that will be beneficial to you? Be willing to move forward.

You should create a *vision for both your personal and business life*. Set the stage for your vision by developing clarity about what you desire. Learn what it takes to be an effective leader. These qualities are especially important in business, but they apply just as well to your personal life.

The *relationships you establish in your personal and business life* will have a great influence on how easily you are able to target your potential. Recognize all the psychological issues that create obstacles in your relationships with friends, family, and your significant other. Understand the importance of creating functional relationships with co-workers and associates. Make sure that you set priorities when networking or socializing so that your own goals can be met without taking second place to everyone else's needs. Make rational decisions about where you choose to invest your energies in these areas.

TARGETING YOUR POTENTIAL WITH A FEARLESS ATTITUDE is about developing an approach to your life. Chances are you won't always be successful, but this is part of the learning process, part of the journey. Don't let your setbacks determine the trend of your life. Use them to regroup, reassess, and move forward once again.

We sincerely hope that sharing these ideas with you has helped you on your journey in some way. We thank you for letting us be part of your journey!

Dannye Williamsen
John Dean Williamsen

ABOUT THE AUTHORS

Dannye Williamsen is an author, editor, and counselor. Her professional background in management in such diverse fields as commodity trading, the cable television industry, and land development has earned her inclusion in Marquis' Chronicles of Human Achievement every year since 2002 in the following: Who's Who in America™, Who's Who of American Women™, and Who's Who in the World™, as well as in Who's Who in Finance and Business™ in 2009-2010. An author and ordained Unity minister, John Dean Williamsen also successfully operated a dental laboratory for many years.

Their company, Williamsen Publications, has published several nonfiction products related to spiritual psychology as well as four novels.

On the next pages, you will find information on these products.

It's Your Move!
Transform Your Dreams From Wishful Thinking To Reality

By Dannye and John Dean Williamsen

5 CD Audio book; Bronze Award in ForeWord Magazine's 2004 Book of the Year Awards

Just because an approach worked for someone else doesn't mean that it's going to work for you! You are unique! Your background, your relationships, your education, your experiences all contribute to a wonderfully unique YOU. They influence your thinking and the way you approach the systems that are supposed to make you successful. Most important, however, you need a system that allows you to master your intentions.

When you create goals in your life that are expressions of your life intentions, you not only experience greater joy and greater prosperity, but you are taking a path that will bring you full circle to the understanding of how unique you REALLY ARE! Who are you behind all those erroneous thoughts about yourself? You are a powerful, creative being! To use this power for its greatest purpose, you have to be aware of your creations.

You cannot discover your life's purpose without becoming a conscious creator. This brings us back to finding the best method for doing this. You're not looking for a Life Method. You need a method that is spiritually based and allows you to work effectively with your inner psychology.

You need a method that is the driving force behind the Law of Attraction. In our 5 CD audio book It's Your Move! *Transform Your Dreams From Wishful Thinking To Reality*, we offer you a process that is outlined in sacred texts back to ancient times. However, the messages, such as those in the parables, are often esoteric or hidden beneath the surface circumstances. It was given this way for those who are ready to dig deeper and take on the mantle of Spirit.

The 7-step creative process in this audio book is the esoteric engine that will move your dreams forward! This is the process that enables you to work on letting go of all that isn't serving you. It helps you manifest the goals that express your Life Intentions. Every time you use it, you hone your skills and enhance your inherent abilities – all of which takes you closer and closer to your ultimate goal:

- being at one with the understanding that you and God are One,
- accepting your creative birthright and mastering your Life Intentions, and
- consciously co-creating with God.

These 5 CDs offer you much more than just the creative process! **It's Your Move!** outlines pitfalls you may encounter & offers you strategies for overcoming them. What's on the CDs? Good question!

CDs #1 and #2 (The Rules) outline for you the seven steps of the creative process. You're already using this process, but because you're not aware of it, your results are hit-and-miss! Sometimes you hit the jackpot! Sometimes you don't. After listening to just these two CDs, you'll better understand how to start taking charge of your dreams.

CD #3 (The Game Pieces) teaches you about the twelve attributes that contribute to your success with the steps of the creative process. The more you hone your skills with these attributes, the greater the harmony in your life.

CDs #4 and #5 (The Game Itself) address your spiritual psychology. What good is it to know how the system works and what you need to make it work better if you don't apply it in your life? Or worse - if you walk blindly into it, unprepared for the pitfalls. These two CDs tell you about the pitfalls and suggest strategies that have worked for others for centuries.

Audio Book: http://www.williamsenpublications.com/ and http://www.amazon.com/Transform-Dreams-Wishful-Thinking-Reality/dp/0972605800.

Metaphysical Minute — *Philosophy on the Run*

By Dannye Williamsen

This book originated as an answer to a need I experienced when I first began to understand that I was a "spiritual being having a human experience" as Teilhard so wonderfully expressed it. As in many fields, it seemed that those who were familiar with the terminology didn't always slow down long enough to discuss the basic ideas with the newly arrived. Two decades later in 2002, I found myself writing those essays myself. At the time, it seemed the best place to share them was online. So early in 2003, I started an e-newsletter with the same name as this book and published a new issue each week for over a year. A paperback was published in 2007 at the request of my subscribers.

It is my hope that my thoughts and experiences will resonate with you and encourage you to express your own in the journal pages provided in the paperback version and in your personal journal if you have the Kindle version. Essays, such as mine, should serve only as a catalyst for your own thoughts—for it is only through thinking and feeling for yourself that you can truly grow in understanding.

Paperback: http://www.WilliamsenPublications.com

Also available as Kindle: http://www.amazon.com/Metaphysical-Minute-Philosophy-Dannye-Williamsen-ebook/dp/B008H4QG36

The 12-Step Business Plan for the Solopreneur

By Dannye Williamsen

This book was *not* written to help you create a business plan for the bank or investors. *The 12-Step Business Plan for the Solopreneur* was written to help you clarify 1) where you want to go, 2) how you plan to get there, and 3) who you want to be when you arrive.

It is a mental check-up, which is the perfect place to start because everything depends on the CLARITY OF YOUR VISION for your business.

Once you have clarified your vision, you will want to move your vision into reality with the creative process with "The Creative Model for the Solopreneur," which is a 12-week intensive.

Paperback: http://www.amazon.com/The-12-Step-Business-Plan-Solopreneur/dp/1453611223/   Also available on Kindle.

The Creative Model for the Solopreneur

By Dannye Williamsen

The Creative Model for the Solopreneur teaches you the underlying principles for success in ANY business or project. Execution with intention of these principles will increase your current achievements, inject new energy into your business and your life, and enable you to better achieve your dreams. You will discover how to use the 7 steps of the creative process, a process that is so incredibly powerful that you will wonder why you haven't heard about it before.

This process is the operation that lies behind the Law of Attraction. It is how you work with the Law of Attraction. The Law is a force. It works with what is in your mind and feelings. This process is what allows you to **refine** the thoughts and feelings that determine what the Law of Attraction uses. Conflicting thoughts and feelings are the reason that we don't always get what we want. It's time to clean up your act – so to speak. Use the process that the Universe has provided to clarify your desires so **the vision for your business can manifest in full bloom.**

Paperback: http://www.amazon.com/The-Creative-Model-Solopreneur-Process/dp/1466262079/

The 4 Cs of Problem-Solving

By John Dean Williamsen

In 1 Hour You'll Discover An Incredible Method You Can Use To Change Your Life Forever!

Problems can be a blessing or a curse! Not knowing how to deal with problems is what causes wallowing and the "poor me" syndrome. So stop wallowing in your problems and start winning by learning this *incredible* method for dealing with any kind of problem.

The **4 Cs method** is based on Universal principles and will blow your mind by how easy it is to remember even when you're knee-deep in negativity. It only takes a moment of clarity to start the method and move toward resolution. So, take an hour of your time to learn a method that will stay with you forever and help you through what you used to think were insurmountable difficulties!

The 4 Cs method will...

- **SHIFT YOUR PERSPECTIVE** from the negative to the positive
- **ADDRESS ANY ISSUES** in the workplace or your life
- **UPGRADE YOUR INTERACTIONS** with others — work, family, or friends
- **BUILD CONFIDENCE** in your ability to think creatively and to follow-through
- **CREATE A COLLABORATIVE ENVIRONMENT** to enhance your productivity.

The emphasis in this method of "problem-solving" is not on the problem itself. It's on the *opportunity it presents for you to determine the flaws in your thinking that need to be cleared in order to reach your goal.*

The OBSTACLE most of us face when a problem arises is having the focus or the strength to rise out of the mire so that we can see clearly. This method shows you how to do this.

Targeting Your Potential

CD Available: http://www.amazon.com/The-Problem-Solving-John-Dean-Williamsen/dp/B003V5WIRY/

Simplicity for the Soul

By John Dean Williamsen

Meditation is not always as easy as some people say it is. Your thoughts can run wild like horses across the plains. Your body can feel like you're sitting on an ant hill. It takes practice and consistency to master your body and your thoughts so that you can benefit from your time in the quiet.

Simplicity for the Soul makes it easy for you to get started and to have some powerful experiences! Being able to experience the relaxation tutorial as often as you like is a bonus if you have trouble letting go of the day's worries.

Learn how to relax with a tutorial on relaxation.

Tame your wild thoughts with the help of these guided meditations.

1) Handful of Clay
2) The Eagle
3) The Corridor

CD Available: http://www.amazon.com/Simplicity-Soul-Rev-John-Williamsen/dp/B003ZK503E/

The Living Organism Called Church

By John Dean Williamsen

A church is a living organism. It is formed by the collective consciousness that emerges from the coming together of those who participate in it. In this incredible message, learn how to recognize the signs that your church is falling victim to the erroneous thoughts and feelings of its members.

The consciousness of a church can experience the challenge of letting go of an old ministry and resurrecting or emerging into a new ministry in the same way we as individuals experience the letting go of old attitudes in order to embrace new ones.

The church can face the challenge of risking the status quo in terms of size or the way things are done so that it can enter a new phase in its growth. The status quo will always try to maintain itself, to resist change. The members of this organism called church are charged with seeking spiritual growth as a group with the same intensity required when seeking their own evolvement if they hope to have a healthy organization.

CD Available:
http://www.williamsenpublications.com/store/p2/The_Living_Organism_Called_Church_.html

The Seasons of My Soul: A Poetic Diary

By Dannye Williamsen

 I wouldn't begin to pretend that these poems have any value to the literary world because I'm quite sure they don't. They were simply my way of expressing the emotions that were overtaking me at different times in my life and yet filling me with wonder at other times.

 I won't apologize if their structure falls short because these "poems" were my safety valve — the outlet that let me release my unproductive emotions. They were also the way I was able to express my personal growth when those around me did not see things the same way I did. So, I bless them … warts and all!

 As you read the poems, you will notice that I have given you the date each was actually written, beginning in 1963 when I was 14 years old. I also shared the event or attitude that sparked the poem.

 At the top of each poem, you will see a running commentary. It is psychological in nature. With hindsight and hopefully greater wisdom, I have tried to present an inner perspective, showing my true journey from 1963 to the final poem I wrote when I reached 50.

 Friends who have read my compilation have uniformly told me that even though I had different experiences than some of them did, they still recognized the emotions behind the different poems. Some evoked memories while others stirred up emotions they thought they had resolved.

 Whatever their effect on you, please know that I lay no claim to being a poet. I do believe, however, that we are all one, struggling to express ourselves and experiencing the same emotions with differing circumstances. If my journey can help you in any way, I am simply grateful.

Targeting Your Potential

Paperback: http://www.amazon.com/Seasons-My-Soul-Poetic-Diary/dp/0972605843/   Also available on Kindle.

Moving on from our passion for spiritual psychology to our passion for writing fiction.

Second Chances

By Dannye Williamsen

Paranormal Suspense, 312 pages.

Guided by Avatar, the wolf, Freddie, whose obsession for control has held her powers in check for years, welcomes them as she faces a battle with her rage-filled ghostly stalker. Will she get a second chance to live and love?

Starting life in an orphanage, Darian slips into a world of perversity when adopted by Harry and Ruth Beel. Kindled by the rage his life has engendered, his inherent powers begin to grow. His obsession to become at one with the Power leads him to a woman he believes is the key.

Fredrika Marsh has led a quiet, controlled life, her only risks being her work as a technical analyst and her friendship with her quirky friend Jodi. Then chaos appears in the ghostly visage of a man who threatens her and, ultimately, her friends.

Avatar, the wolf, after nearly losing his life force to Darian and sensing the innocent somehow connected to this monster, is dedicated to helping Fredrika survive the dark power that drives Darian by encouraging her to embrace her own power.

Every corner of Fredrika's life is invaded, her self-sufficiency lost. She must trust others to survive. Most of all, she must risk trusting herself, for the paranormal ability she fears is the only way she can survive. Her search for answers brings Garrison McCrary into her life, raising the question: *will she get a second chance--a chance to live and to love?*

Targeting Your Potential

Paperback: http://www.amazon.com/Second-Chances-Dannye-Williamsen/dp/097260586X/   Also available on Kindle.

The Threads That Bind

By Dannye Williamsen

Paranormal Suspense, 326 pages.

Thirty-nine years later, the threads that bind the generations begin to reconnect for the final battle in *The Threads That Bind*, the sequel to *Second Chances*.

By quirk of fate, Mandy Gray, whose last and best friend was Fredrika Marsh, leaves her secluded profession as a research psychologist in 2019 to take a position as a guidance counselor at Briarton Academy where the orphaned and wealthy Jillian Missildine is a student. They become fast friends, but it is four years before they discover the thread that connects them.

Once this connection is made, all the others — those connected to the past through Freddie and her nemesis — flow swiftly toward each other. The patterns of their lives become tangled and knotted, and the decision has to be made about who will survive.

"Sometimes the threads of one's life fit neatly together and a pattern begins to emerge that has great promise. Other times, the threads become tangled and knotted, and the pattern gets lost. When this happens, it is best to snip the threads and begin again, for the pattern always awaits you."
— ©The Book of Metanoia

Available: http://www.amazon.com/Threads-That-Bind-Dannye-Williamsen/dp/0972605878/   Also available on Kindle.

Center Stage

By Dannye Williamsen

Paranormal Romance: 204 pages.

    Have you ever looked back over your life and wondered what would have happened if you had made a different choice along the way? April Saunders never even considered it until her life spun out of control and she was alone. When she is offered the chance of a lifetime, her obsessive desire to be center stage blinds her to other possibilities. Can there be salvation for one who has betrayed so many?

Available: http://www.amazon.com/Center-Stage-Dannye-Williamsen/dp/0972605835/   Also available on Kindle.

The Evolution of a Slingshot

By John Dean Williamsen

Coming-of-age / murder mystery, 272 pages.

The Evolution of a Slingshot is a story of a boy whose life is often as raw and unfettered as the times. He lives in a world of tarpaper shacks and basement homes, of dusty roads and outhouses, of poverty and optimism, of the American Dream and justice snubbed.

In the late 1940s, while the country is recovering from the Great Depression and World War II, an eleven-year-old boy is simply trying to survive his small town world in Illinois. The great tragedy in his life has been the mysterious murder of his father, which has turned his world upside-down. The fear that grows out of his loss leads him to cling to his brother, Ray, as a substitute father figure. Unfortunately, Ray is only four years older, and while seeking retribution for his father's death, he is also struggling with his family's expectations of his filling his father's shoes.

After watching the way Ray handles the situation when Jake is attacked on his paper route, Jake recognizes how self-destructive his brother's anger can be, and he is afraid for him. This strengthens Jake's resolve to handle his problems himself. The slingshot, which was once a toy to Jake, has now become his only means of defense. His life continues to offer him opportunities to choose how to deal with confrontations and the loss of others close to him.

His struggle to make the right choices transforms his relationship with his slingshot. It is this evolving relationship that mirrors the changes in Jake's inner psychology—the changes which mold his personality and shape his ideas of right and wrong. When he finds himself at the decisive moment where he has the means to avenge the wrongs his family has suffered, what will his decision be? His future now hinges on the choices he makes.

Available: http://www.amazon.com/Evolution-Slingshot-Toy-Catalyst-Change/dp/1479302503/ Also available on Kindle.

www.ingramcontent.com/pod-product-compliance
Lightning Source LLC
Chambersburg PA
CBHW072343100426
42738CB00049B/1462